Mastering Large Language Models

Copyright © 2025

This text is designed to provide accurate and reliable information about the subject matter it covers. The publisher sells it without promising to provide specialized services like accounting or legal advice. If such professional guidance is needed, one should consult a qualified expert in that field.

This content is based on a set of principles endorsed by both a committee from the American Bar Association and one from a group of Publishers and Associations. Reproducing, copying, or sharing any part of this document through electronic or printed means is illegal. Recording or storing this publication without the publisher's written consent is strictly forbidden. All rights are reserved. The information given is believed to be honest and stable, with the understanding that any liability for negligence or otherwise, arising from the use or misuse of any information, policies, or instructions in this document, lies entirely with the reader. The publisher is not liable for any losses or damages, direct or indirect, that may result from the use of the information provided. Copyrights not held by the publisher belong to the respective authors. The information is meant for informational purposes only and is not presented with any guarantee or warranty. Trademarks mentioned are used without permission, and their publication does not imply endorsement by the trademark owner. All trademarks and brands mentioned in this book are used for identification purposes only and belong to their respective owners, not associated with this publication.

Mastering Large Language Models

A Hands-On Guide to AI-Powered Applications, Cutting-Edge Techniques for LLM Engineering, Fine-Tuning, and Scalable Deployment

Geoff L. Parks

Table of Contents

Introduction 8
    Chapter 1: Welcome to the World of LLMs 8
        Why Large Language Models Are Transforming AI 8
        The Rise of LLM-Powered Applications 10
        Who This Book Is For: Your Journey with LLMs 13
    Chapter 2: How to Use This Book 16
        Learning Roadmap: From Fundamentals to Advanced Applications 16
        Tools and Resources You'll Need 18

Part 1: Foundations of Large Language Models 20
    Chapter 3: Understanding LLMs: The Core Concepts 20
        What Are LLMs and How Do They Work? 20
        LLM Architecture: Encoders, Decoders, and Attention Mechanisms 23
        Key Players: GPT, Llama, Falcon, and Beyond 26
    Chapter 4: Building Blocks of LLM Applications 30
        The Role of Data: Embeddings, Tokenization, and Context 30
        Exploring Pretrained Models vs. Building from Scratch 33
        Ethical Considerations and Responsible AI 36

Part 2: Practical Applications of LLMs 41
    Chapter 5: Prompt Engineering: Unlocking the True Power of LLMs 41
        The Science of Crafting Prompts 41
        Techniques: Few-Shot Learning, Chain-of-Thought Prompting, and RAG 44
        Common Mistakes and How to Avoid Them 48
    Chapter 6: LLMs in Real-World Applications 52
        Building Conversational AI for Business 52
        Creating Search and Recommendation Engines 56
        Using LLMs with Structured and Unstructured Data 60

Part 3: Hands-On Development 66
    Chapter 7: Designing and Training Your Own LLM 66
        Step-by-Step Guide to LLM Development 66
        Preparing Datasets for Pretraining and Fine-Tuning 70
        Hands-On Implementation with Python and PyTorch 75

- Chapter 8: Fine-Tuning for Specific Tasks 81
  - Supervised Fine-Tuning and Preference Alignment 81
  - Leveraging Transfer Learning for Efficiency 86
  - Case Study: Customizing an LLM for Your Needs 90

Part 4: Deploying LLMs for Production 96

- Chapter 9: From Prototype to Production 96
  - Creating Scalable and Modular LLM Solutions 96
  - Infrastructure as Code (IaC) with AWS and Other Tools 101
  - Continuous Training and Monitoring for Performance 108
- Chapter 10: Optimizing LLMs for Efficiency 114
  - Inference Optimization: Speed and Cost Reduction 114
  - RAG Pipelines for Real-Time Data Ingestion 120
  - Leveraging Vector Databases and Non-Parametric Knowledge 125

Part 5: Advanced Topics and Innovations 131

- Chapter 11: Beyond Text: Building Multimodal Applications 131
  - The Emergence of Foundation Models (LFMs) 136
- Chapter 12: Emerging Trends in LLMs 142
  - The Future of AI with LLMs 142
  - Ethical AI: Challenges and Solutions 146
  - Innovations on the Horizon 152

Conclusion 157

- Chapter 13: Your Path Forward 157
  - Tips for Continuous Learning and Staying Ahead 161
  - Leveraging LLM Skills for Career Growth 166

FREE SUPPLEMENTARY RESOURCES

☑ LLM REAL WORLD SCENARIOS
☑ LLM SOLUTIONS AND CODE EXAMPLES

SCAN THE QR CODE TO DOWNLOAD

COMPLEMENTARY RESOURCES

Why Your Support Matters for This Book:

Creating this book has been an unexpectedly tough journey, more so than even the most complex coding sessions. For the first time, I've faced the daunting challenge of writer's block. While I understand the subject matter, translating it into clear, logical, and engaging writing is another matter altogether.
Moreover, my choice to bypass traditional publishers has led me to embrace the role of an 'independent author.' This path has had its hurdles, yet my commitment to helping others remains strong.
This is why your feedback on Amazon would be incredibly valuable. Your thoughts and opinions not only matter greatly to me, but they also play a crucial role in spreading the word about this book. Here's what I suggest:

1. If you haven't done so already, scan the QR code at the beginning of the book to download the FREE SUPPLEMENTARY RESOURCES.

2. Scan the QR code below and quickly leave feedback on Amazon!

The optimal approach? Consider making a brief video to share your impressions of the book! If that's a bit much, don't worry at all. Just leaving a feedback and including a few photos of the book would be fantastic too!

Note: There's no obligation whatsoever, but it would be immensely valued!

I'm thrilled to embark on this journey with you. Are you prepared to delve in?
Enjoy your reading!

Introduction

Chapter 1: Welcome to the World of LLMs

Why Large Language Models Are Transforming AI

Large Language Models (LLMs) have emerged as transformative forces in artificial intelligence (AI), revolutionizing the way machines understand, generate, and interact with human language. From powering conversational agents to enabling advanced research capabilities, LLMs are reshaping industries and redefining the limits of what AI can achieve. But why exactly are these models at the forefront of AI transformation? To answer this, we must delve into their architecture, capabilities, and the unprecedented applications they enable.

The Foundation of Large Language Models

At their core, LLMs are deep learning systems designed to process and generate natural language. These models are built on transformer architectures, which were introduced by Vaswani et al. in 2017 through the groundbreaking paper "Attention Is All You Need." Transformers rely on self-attention mechanisms, allowing models to weigh the importance of different words in a sequence relative to one another. This architecture enables LLMs to capture context more effectively than previous approaches, such as recurrent neural networks (RNNs) or long short-term memory (LSTM) networks.

The ability to handle massive amounts of data is another defining feature of LLMs. They are trained on terabytes of text data scraped from diverse sources, including books, websites, and academic articles. This training provides LLMs with a broad knowledge base, enabling them to understand and generate text in multiple languages, answer complex questions, and even perform specialized tasks without domain-specific fine-tuning. The scale of training data, coupled with billions or even trillions of parameters, allows LLMs to model intricate language patterns and subtle nuances in communication.

Bridging the Gap Between Machines and Humans

One of the most compelling reasons LLMs are transforming AI is their ability to bridge the gap between human and machine communication. Historically, interactions with computers have been limited to rigid, predefined commands. LLMs, however, enable more natural and intuitive exchanges, akin to human conversation. This shift is particularly evident in the proliferation of chatbots and virtual assistants, such as OpenAI's ChatGPT, Google's Bard, and Microsoft's integration of GPT models into its products.

These systems can comprehend and generate coherent responses, making them invaluable for customer support, education, and personal productivity. For instance, a student can use an LLM-powered assistant to learn complex topics by asking questions in natural language, while a business professional might rely on such tools to draft emails or summarize lengthy documents. This democratization of access to advanced language capabilities is revolutionizing how individuals and organizations operate.

Advancing Knowledge and Creativity

Beyond facilitating better communication, LLMs are also enhancing knowledge discovery and creativity. Their ability to analyze vast amounts of text data and generate meaningful insights has made them indispensable in fields like medicine, law, and scientific research. For example, LLMs can assist researchers in literature reviews by summarizing thousands of articles or suggesting novel research directions based on existing studies. In medicine, they have been employed to draft patient reports, recommend treatment plans, and even hypothesize potential drug interactions.

Creativity, once considered a uniquely human domain, is another area where LLMs excel. From generating poetry and music lyrics to assisting in screenwriting, these models are helping creators overcome writer's block and explore new artistic territories. Tools like OpenAI's DALL•E, which generates images from textual descriptions, exemplify how LLMs can transcend language to inspire creativity across multiple modalities.

Democratizing Technology

The accessibility of LLMs is another factor driving their transformative impact. Previously, advanced AI systems were confined to elite institutions with significant computational resources. Today, open-source initiatives and cloud-based platforms have made LLMs accessible to a broader audience. Models like GPT-3, GPT-4, Llama 2, and Falcon LLM are available to developers, researchers, and businesses, enabling them to integrate sophisticated language capabilities into their products without the need to build models from scratch.

This democratization is particularly empowering for small businesses and startups, which can now leverage LLMs to compete with larger corporations. Whether it's automating customer interactions, personalizing marketing strategies, or enhancing product design, these tools provide cost-effective solutions that were previously unattainable. By lowering the barrier to entry, LLMs are fostering innovation and leveling the playing field across industries.

Addressing Multimodal Challenges

While language remains the primary focus of LLMs, their capabilities are expanding into multimodal domains that integrate text, vision, and audio. This evolution is paving the way for applications that go beyond traditional text-based interactions. For example, models like OpenAI's GPT-4 and Meta's research into foundation models are exploring how LLMs can process and generate data across multiple modalities.

Imagine a scenario where a doctor can input patient symptoms (text) and medical imaging data (visual) into an AI system that then provides a comprehensive diagnosis and treatment plan. Similarly, content creators can use multimodal LLMs to generate both textual and visual assets for marketing campaigns. By breaking down silos between different data types, LLMs are unlocking new possibilities in how humans interact with and derive value from AI systems.

Ethical Considerations and Challenges

Despite their transformative potential, LLMs also raise significant ethical and practical challenges. Issues such as bias, misinformation, and misuse of AI-generated content are pressing concerns. Because these models learn from large datasets that may contain biased or harmful content, they can inadvertently perpetuate stereotypes or generate inappropriate outputs.

Furthermore, the ability of LLMs to produce human-like text has sparked debates about the authenticity and reliability of information. Deepfake text—content designed to deceive—can be used for malicious purposes, such as spreading disinformation or conducting phishing attacks. Addressing these challenges requires robust ethical guidelines, transparency in model development, and the implementation of safeguards to detect and mitigate harmful outputs.

Economic and Societal Impacts

The widespread adoption of LLMs is also reshaping the economic landscape. By automating repetitive tasks and enhancing productivity, these models are enabling businesses to streamline operations and reduce costs. For example, LLMs can automate data entry, generate reports, and even code software, freeing up human resources for more strategic and creative endeavors.

However, this shift also raises concerns about job displacement and the need for workforce reskilling. As LLMs take over certain roles, individuals and organizations must adapt by acquiring new skills and exploring opportunities in AI-driven industries. Education and training programs that focus on AI literacy will be crucial in ensuring a smooth transition and minimizing societal disruptions.

The Future of LLMs

The trajectory of LLMs suggests a future where AI systems are deeply integrated into every aspect of human life. Advancements in areas like reinforcement learning, preference alignment, and continuous learning will further enhance their capabilities, making them even more adaptive and reliable. Innovations such as parameter-efficient fine-tuning methods, like LoRA (Low-Rank Adaptation), are also making it easier to customize LLMs for specific tasks without requiring extensive computational resources.

As LLMs evolve, their role in fostering collaboration between humans and machines will become increasingly prominent. These systems will not replace human intelligence but will augment it, providing tools and insights that enhance decision-making, creativity, and problem-solving. By embracing these advancements, individuals and organizations can unlock the full potential of AI to address complex challenges and drive progress.

Conclusion

Large Language Models are not just technological advancements; they are paradigm shifts in how we interact with information and technology. Their ability to understand, generate, and apply human language at an unprecedented scale is transforming industries, democratizing access to advanced tools, and opening new frontiers in knowledge and creativity. While challenges remain, the potential benefits far outweigh the risks, making LLMs a cornerstone of the AI revolution. By understanding and leveraging these models, we stand at the brink of a future where human ingenuity and machine intelligence work hand in hand to shape a better world.

The Rise of LLM-Powered Applications

The rise of large language model (LLM)-powered applications marks a turning point in the evolution of artificial intelligence (AI), unlocking capabilities that were once considered the stuff of science fiction. From powering conversational agents to enhancing creative workflows, LLMs are driving innovations across industries and redefining how businesses and individuals engage with technology. Their versatility, scalability, and ability to deliver context-aware responses are propelling them to the forefront of the AI revolution. This chapter explores the transformative impact of LLM-powered applications and the diverse roles they play in shaping the future of technology.

The Roots of LLM Applications

To understand the meteoric rise of LLM-powered applications, it is essential to trace their origins. Large language models, such as OpenAI's GPT series, Google's Bard, and Meta's Llama 2, were initially conceptualized as tools to improve natural language understanding and generation. Their early implementations focused on tasks like sentiment analysis, translation, and text summarization. However, as the models grew in scale and sophistication, their potential expanded exponentially.

The turning point came with the development of transformer architectures, which introduced mechanisms like self-attention to efficiently process long sequences of text. These innovations enabled LLMs to capture nuanced linguistic relationships, giving rise to applications capable of generating human-like text, understanding context, and solving complex problems. This technological leap not only enhanced existing applications but also laid the groundwork for entirely new use cases.

Expanding Horizons: LLMs in Business and Industry

One of the most visible impacts of LLMs has been their adoption in business environments. Enterprises across sectors are leveraging LLM-powered applications to streamline operations, improve customer interactions, and enhance decision-making processes. For example, companies are using chatbots and virtual assistants to provide round-the-clock customer support, answer frequently asked questions, and guide users through complex processes. These systems—built on LLM frameworks—are not just reactive but proactive, predicting user needs and delivering tailored solutions.

In the healthcare industry, LLMs are revolutionizing patient care and administrative workflows. Applications include automating the creation of medical reports, summarizing patient histories, and even assisting in diagnosing illnesses by analyzing symptoms described in natural language. These tools enable healthcare professionals to focus on direct patient care while reducing the time spent on routine documentation tasks.

In finance, LLMs are being used to analyze market trends, generate reports, and even detect fraudulent activities. For instance, financial advisors are employing AI-driven insights to create personalized investment strategies, while banks are leveraging LLMs for risk assessment and compliance monitoring. The ability of these models to process and analyze vast amounts of unstructured data is proving invaluable in decision-making and strategic planning.

Creativity Unleashed: LLMs in Content Creation

Another area where LLM-powered applications are making waves is content creation. Writers, marketers, and designers are using these models to draft articles, generate ad copy, and brainstorm creative concepts. Platforms like Jasper AI and Copy.ai, powered by GPT models, are helping professionals produce high-quality content faster and more efficiently.

LLMs are not just limited to textual content. They are also driving advancements in multimedia applications. For example, combining LLMs with image generation models, such as DALL•E, allows users to create stunning visuals from simple text prompts. This synergy is empowering creators to explore new artistic directions and expand their creative horizons.

Additionally, LLMs are being used in entertainment and gaming. Game developers are integrating these models to generate dynamic storylines, dialogue, and character interactions, creating more immersive experiences for players. In film and television, scriptwriters are experimenting with LLMs to co-write screenplays or develop plotlines, highlighting how AI can complement human creativity.

Education and Learning: A Personalized Approach

The education sector has also embraced LLM-powered applications, using them to deliver personalized learning experiences. Virtual tutors, powered by LLMs, can adapt to individual learning styles, answer questions in real time, and provide detailed explanations tailored to the student's level of understanding. This approach not only enhances accessibility but also ensures that learners receive support that is specifically suited to their needs.

Educational platforms are leveraging LLMs to create adaptive learning modules, generate practice questions, and even assess student performance. These applications are particularly valuable in addressing knowledge gaps and fostering engagement in remote or hybrid learning environments. By providing instant feedback and resources, LLM-powered tools are transforming the way education is delivered and consumed.

LLMs as Collaborative Partners in Coding

In the realm of software development, LLM-powered applications are redefining coding workflows. Tools like GitHub Copilot, built on models such as Codex, assist developers by suggesting code snippets, debugging errors, and automating repetitive tasks. These applications act as collaborative partners, enabling developers to focus on higher-level problem-solving and innovation.

LLMs are also democratizing coding for non-programmers. By interpreting natural language instructions, these models can generate code for basic applications, making software development accessible to a broader audience. This capability is particularly valuable for small businesses and entrepreneurs who lack technical expertise but want to create custom solutions.

Transforming Knowledge Work

Beyond specific industries, LLM-powered applications are reshaping knowledge work more broadly. Professionals in law, journalism, and research are using these models to draft documents, summarize reports, and analyze complex datasets. In legal settings, LLMs assist with contract review and legal research, saving time and reducing errors. In journalism, they help reporters sift through vast amounts of information to uncover key insights and generate concise summaries.

These applications are not merely tools for automation but are also catalysts for innovation. By handling time-consuming tasks, LLMs free up professionals to focus on strategic thinking, creativity, and problem-solving. This shift is driving productivity gains across a wide range of professions.

The Role of LLMs in Accessibility

Another critical area of impact is accessibility. LLM-powered applications are breaking down barriers for individuals with disabilities, enabling more inclusive communication and interaction. For instance, speech-to-text and text-to-speech applications, powered by LLMs, provide seamless translation for individuals with hearing or speech impairments. Additionally, these models are improving access to information for people with visual impairments by generating descriptive text for images and visual content.

Multilingual capabilities are another strength of LLMs, facilitating cross-cultural communication and breaking language barriers. Businesses are using LLM-powered translation tools to expand their global reach, while educators are leveraging these capabilities to provide multilingual resources for students worldwide.

Challenges in Scaling LLM Applications

Despite their transformative potential, LLM-powered applications face challenges in scalability, ethics, and governance. One significant hurdle is the computational cost associated with training and deploying these models. Running LLMs requires substantial resources, including high-performance hardware and vast amounts of energy, raising concerns about sustainability.

Ethical considerations also loom large. Issues such as bias in training data, misinformation, and potential misuse of AI-generated content must be addressed to ensure responsible deployment. Companies developing LLM-powered applications are implementing safeguards, such as content moderation and transparency mechanisms, to mitigate these risks.

Finally, there is the challenge of user trust. While LLMs are highly capable, their outputs are not always accurate or reliable. Ensuring that users understand the limitations of these models is crucial for fostering confidence and promoting responsible use.

The Future of LLM-Powered Applications

Looking ahead, the potential of LLM-powered applications is boundless. As models become more efficient and adaptable, their integration into everyday life will deepen. Innovations in fine-tuning, reinforcement learning, and multimodal capabilities will further enhance their performance and broaden their use cases.

One promising direction is the development of domain-specific LLMs, tailored to excel in specialized fields such as medicine, law, or engineering. These models will offer greater accuracy and relevance, enabling more effective problem-solving in high-stakes environments.

Another exciting prospect is the emergence of multimodal applications that combine text, images, audio, and even real-time sensor data. These advancements will pave the way for more intuitive and immersive AI experiences, transforming how humans interact with technology.

Conclusion

The rise of LLM-powered applications represents a seismic shift in the landscape of artificial intelligence. By enabling more natural, intuitive, and powerful interactions between humans and machines, these applications are driving progress across industries and enriching countless aspects of daily life. While challenges remain, the potential benefits far outweigh the risks, making LLMs a cornerstone of the AI-driven future. As these technologies continue to evolve, their ability to enhance productivity, creativity, and accessibility will solidify their role as indispensable tools in the modern world.

Who This Book Is For: Your Journey with LLMs

Artificial intelligence (AI) has rapidly evolved from a niche field into a transformative force shaping industries and everyday life. Central to this revolution are Large Language Models (LLMs), which have redefined how machines understand, generate, and interact with human language. This book is designed to serve as your companion on a journey into the world of LLMs, equipping you with the knowledge and tools to unlock their full potential. But who exactly is this book for, and how can it guide you? Let us delve into the specific audiences, their goals, and how this book can address their unique needs.

AI Enthusiasts and Newcomers to LLMs

If you are new to the world of artificial intelligence, this book is your gateway to understanding one of the most exciting and impactful technologies of our time. Large Language Models can appear complex and intimidating at first glance, with terms like "transformer architectures" and "inference optimization" potentially sounding arcane. However, this book aims to demystify these concepts and provide a structured learning path that starts with the basics.

You'll gain an understanding of the core principles that underpin LLMs, including how they process language, learn from vast datasets, and generate human-like text. Through real-world examples and clear explanations, this book ensures that even readers with no prior experience in AI can grasp the fundamentals. By the end of your journey, you'll not only appreciate how LLMs work but also feel confident in applying them to solve problems and create innovative solutions.

Professionals Seeking to Integrate LLMs into Their Work

The influence of LLMs is not confined to the tech industry; their applications span a wide range of fields, from healthcare and finance to marketing and education. For professionals who want to harness the power of LLMs to improve their workflows and decision-making processes, this book provides actionable insights and hands-on guidance.

For instance, if you work in marketing, you will learn how LLMs can generate personalized content at scale, analyze consumer sentiment, and optimize ad campaigns. If you are in healthcare, you'll discover how LLMs can assist in drafting patient reports, summarizing medical research, and even providing diagnostic support. Educators will find value in exploring how LLMs can create adaptive learning modules and serve as virtual tutors for personalized instruction.

This book focuses on practical applications, helping you identify opportunities where LLMs can add value in your specific domain. You'll also learn how to implement these technologies responsibly, ensuring that ethical considerations and data privacy are integrated into your deployment strategies.

Software Developers and Engineers

For software developers and engineers, this book serves as both a technical guide and a source of inspiration. Whether you're an experienced AI practitioner or a developer looking to expand your skill set, you'll find the resources and examples needed to build robust LLM-powered applications.

The book delves into the nuts and bolts of working with LLMs, from understanding transformer architectures to fine-tuning models for specific tasks. You'll learn how to integrate LLMs into your existing systems, optimize performance, and create scalable solutions. Hands-on sections guide you through coding examples, making it easier to apply theoretical concepts to real-world projects.

Additionally, this book explores cutting-edge advancements, such as multimodal LLMs that combine text, image, and audio data, and techniques for optimizing inference to reduce computational costs. By the end of your journey, you'll have the expertise to develop applications that not only meet current demands but also anticipate future innovations.

AI Researchers and Academics

For those in academia or research, this book provides a comprehensive overview of the state-of-the-art in LLMs while also offering a springboard for further exploration. Researchers can benefit from detailed discussions on topics like supervised fine-tuning, preference alignment, and reinforcement learning. The book also highlights ongoing challenges and open questions in the field, encouraging you to contribute to advancing LLM technology.

Whether you're studying the ethical implications of AI, investigating new architectures, or exploring domain-specific applications, this book serves as a valuable resource. By consolidating foundational knowledge with insights into emerging trends, it equips you to conduct impactful research and stay ahead in a rapidly evolving field.

Entrepreneurs and Innovators

Entrepreneurs and innovators looking to disrupt industries with cutting-edge AI solutions will find this book particularly valuable. LLMs offer unprecedented opportunities to create applications that were previously unimaginable, from personalized virtual assistants to intelligent recommendation systems.

This book helps you identify high-impact use cases and guides you through the process of building prototypes and scaling solutions. You'll learn about cost-effective strategies for deploying LLMs, including leveraging open-source models and cloud-based services. Additionally, the book discusses practical considerations like user experience design, ethical deployment, and maintaining competitive differentiation in a crowded market.

Lifelong Learners and Curious Minds

For the intellectually curious and lifelong learners, this book is an invitation to explore a transformative technology that is reshaping the way we communicate, create, and collaborate. Whether you're fascinated by the philosophical implications of AI or intrigued by its technical underpinnings, this book offers a balanced blend of conceptual depth and practical insight.

You'll explore questions like: How do machines learn to understand human language? What are the limitations of LLMs, and how can they be addressed? How will this technology impact society in the coming decades? By engaging with these topics, you'll develop a nuanced perspective that goes beyond the hype and headlines.

Addressing Common Concerns

As you embark on this journey, it's natural to have questions and concerns about engaging with a complex and rapidly evolving technology. This book anticipates these anxieties and provides clear, reassuring guidance.

1. **Intimidation by Complexity:** If you feel overwhelmed by the technical jargon or the sheer scale of LLMs, rest assured that this book is designed to break down complex concepts into digestible explanations. Step-by-step tutorials and real-world examples ensure that you can follow along, regardless of your starting point.

2. **Ethical and Privacy Concerns:** Many readers worry about the ethical implications of deploying LLMs, particularly around issues like bias and data security. This book addresses these concerns head-on, offering practical strategies for responsible AI development and deployment.

3. **Fear of Obsolescence:** With technology evolving so quickly, you might wonder if the knowledge you gain today will still be relevant tomorrow. This book emphasizes foundational principles and transferable skills, ensuring that you can adapt to new developments and remain at the cutting edge.

Your Journey with LLMs

By the time you complete this book, you will have not only a deep understanding of Large Language Models but also the confidence to apply this knowledge in meaningful ways. You'll be equipped to:

- Understand the inner workings of LLMs, from their architecture to their training processes.
- Identify and implement practical use cases that align with your personal or professional goals.
- Navigate ethical challenges and deploy LLMs responsibly.
- Stay informed about emerging trends and advancements in AI technology.

Whether you're seeking to enhance your career, launch a groundbreaking application, or simply satisfy your curiosity, this book is your trusted guide to the world of LLMs. Together, we will explore the transformative potential of this technology and empower you to become an active participant in shaping its future.

Chapter 2: How to Use This Book

Understanding the vast and intricate field of Large Language Models (LLMs) can be a daunting task. This book has been carefully structured to provide a clear and logical progression, guiding you from foundational concepts to advanced applications. In this section, we will outline the learning roadmap that underpins this book, ensuring that you can navigate its content effectively and extract maximum value. Additionally, we will discuss the tools and resources you'll need to accompany you on this journey, enabling you to apply the knowledge you gain with confidence.

Learning Roadmap: From Fundamentals to Advanced Applications

The key to mastering any complex subject lies in breaking it down into manageable phases. This book's roadmap is designed to provide a step-by-step journey through the essential components of LLMs, ensuring that you build a robust understanding before diving into advanced topics.

Phase 1: Foundations of Large Language Models

This initial phase focuses on building your foundational knowledge. Whether you're an AI novice or someone with technical expertise, it's crucial to establish a solid grasp of the basic principles that underpin LLMs. In this phase, you will learn:

- **The Evolution of Natural Language Processing (NLP):** Understand how LLMs emerged from earlier approaches in NLP, including rule-based systems, statistical methods, and neural networks.

- **Core Concepts of LLMs:** Explore key ideas like tokenization, embeddings, and attention mechanisms that enable LLMs to process and generate human-like text.

- **Transformer Architectures:** Delve into the architecture that revolutionized AI, with a detailed explanation of how transformers work and why they're superior to earlier models like RNNs and LSTMs.

- **The Training Process:** Learn how LLMs are trained on vast datasets, including pretraining and fine-tuning phases, and the role of hyperparameters in optimizing performance.

This phase lays the groundwork for everything that follows, equipping you with the terminology, principles, and context needed to understand more advanced material.

Phase 2: Practical Applications and Use Cases

Once you've mastered the basics, the next step is to explore how LLMs are applied in real-world scenarios. This phase focuses on practical applications, giving you hands-on experience and showing you how LLMs can be leveraged to solve problems across industries.

- **Prompt Engineering:** Discover how to craft effective prompts to maximize the output quality of LLMs. Techniques like few-shot learning and chain-of-thought prompting will be covered.

- **Building Chatbots and Virtual Assistants:** Learn how to design conversational AI systems for customer support, personal productivity, or educational purposes.

- **Text Summarization and Content Generation:** Explore use cases like automated report writing, article summarization, and creative writing assistance.
- **Industry-Specific Applications:** Understand how LLMs are transforming fields such as healthcare, finance, marketing, and education.

By the end of this phase, you'll be able to identify and implement LLM-powered solutions tailored to your specific needs or interests.

Phase 3: Developing and Customizing LLMs

This phase takes you deeper into the technical aspects of LLMs, enabling you to customize and optimize models for specialized tasks. It's aimed at readers with a technical background who want to move beyond using pre-trained models.

- **Fine-Tuning LLMs:** Learn how to adapt pre-trained models to domain-specific applications by retraining them on targeted datasets.
- **Data Engineering for LLMs:** Explore techniques for preparing high-quality datasets, including cleaning, annotating, and managing large-scale data pipelines.
- **Multimodal Integration:** Discover how to extend LLM capabilities to handle inputs and outputs beyond text, such as integrating image and audio processing.
- **Optimization Techniques:** Delve into strategies like inference optimization, parameter-efficient fine-tuning (e.g., LoRA), and reducing computational costs.

This phase provides the technical depth required to unlock the full potential of LLMs, allowing you to push the boundaries of what these models can achieve.

Phase 4: Advanced Topics and Emerging Trends

The final phase of the roadmap is dedicated to exploring cutting-edge advancements and addressing broader implications of LLMs in society.

- **Ethical Considerations:** Examine challenges like bias, misinformation, and privacy concerns, and learn how to deploy LLMs responsibly.
- **Reinforcement Learning with Human Feedback (RLHF):** Understand how this technique improves the alignment of LLM outputs with human intentions.
- **Emerging Trends:** Stay ahead of the curve by exploring innovations such as foundation models, continual learning, and real-time data integration.
- **Future Directions:** Reflect on the evolving landscape of LLMs and their potential to transform industries and society.

By the end of this phase, you'll not only have a comprehensive understanding of LLMs but also a forward-looking perspective on their future applications and challenges.

Tools and Resources You'll Need

While the learning roadmap provides a clear path, the right tools and resources are essential for putting theory into practice. Below, we outline the software, platforms, and materials you'll need to accompany you on your journey.

Computing Resources

- **Laptop or Desktop Computer:** A modern computer with at least 16GB of RAM and a dedicated GPU (optional but recommended) is ideal for experimenting with LLMs.

- **Cloud Services:** Platforms like Google Colab, AWS, or Microsoft Azure provide cloud-based resources for running LLMs. Google Colab is particularly useful for beginners due to its free tier and ease of use.

Programming Environment

- **Python:** The dominant programming language for AI and LLM development. Ensure you have Python 3.7 or later installed.

- **Integrated Development Environment (IDE):** Tools like Visual Studio Code or Jupyter Notebook are excellent for writing and testing code.

AI Frameworks and Libraries

- **PyTorch or TensorFlow:** These are the leading deep learning frameworks. PyTorch is often preferred for its ease of use and flexibility in research and development.

- **Hugging Face Transformers Library:** A powerful and user-friendly library for working with pre-trained LLMs, including GPT, BERT, and more.

- **LangChain:** A framework designed to build applications powered by LLMs, especially for orchestrating multi-step workflows.

Datasets

- **Open Datasets:** Platforms like Kaggle, Hugging Face Datasets, and Google Dataset Search provide access to diverse datasets for training and fine-tuning models.

- **Custom Data:** For domain-specific applications, you may need to collect and preprocess your own datasets. Tools like pandas and NLTK can help with data manipulation and analysis.

Collaboration and Version Control

- **Git and GitHub:** Essential tools for version control and collaboration, allowing you to track changes and work with others on shared projects.

Learning and Documentation

- **Official Documentation:** Always refer to the official documentation for libraries and frameworks, such as PyTorch or Hugging Face.

- **Tutorials and Online Courses:** Platforms like Coursera, Udemy, and YouTube offer excellent tutorials on LLM concepts and implementation.

- **Books and Research Papers:** Supplement your learning with foundational texts and recent research articles to deepen your understanding.

Community and Support

- **Forums and Online Communities:** Join platforms like Stack Overflow, Reddit (e.g., r/MachineLearning), and Hugging Face's community forums for support and discussion.
- **Local Meetups and Conferences:** Attend AI-focused events to network with professionals and learn from industry leaders.

Experimentation Tools

- **Sandbox Environments:** Use environments like Google Colab for experimentation and prototyping without the need for extensive local resources.
- **Visualization Tools:** Libraries like Matplotlib and Seaborn are invaluable for visualizing data and model performance.

Maximizing the Tools and Resources

To make the most of these tools and resources, it's important to approach your learning journey with a mindset of exploration and experimentation. Don't be afraid to try new techniques, tweak existing models, and learn from failures. Combine theoretical knowledge with practical application, and leverage the wealth of online resources and communities to accelerate your progress.

By following this roadmap and utilizing the recommended tools and resources, you'll be well-equipped to navigate the world of LLMs. Whether you're a beginner exploring AI for the first time or an experienced professional looking to deepen your expertise, this book provides the structure and guidance needed to achieve your goals.

Part 1: Foundations of Large Language Models

Chapter 3: Understanding LLMs: The Core Concepts

What Are LLMs and How Do They Work?

Large Language Models (LLMs) represent a groundbreaking advancement in artificial intelligence, designed to understand, generate, and interact with human language at an unprecedented scale. These models have revolutionized fields ranging from natural language processing (NLP) to creative writing and problem-solving, enabling machines to produce human-like text, comprehend nuanced queries, and assist in complex tasks. But what exactly are LLMs, and how do they work? To fully appreciate their transformative potential, it is essential to delve into their definition, underlying principles, and operational mechanics.

What Are LLMs?

At their core, Large Language Models are advanced neural networks trained on massive datasets to perform a wide range of language-related tasks. These tasks include text generation, summarization, translation, question answering, and more. The defining feature of LLMs is their sheer scale, characterized by billions or even trillions of parameters—the adjustable weights that determine the model's behavior.

The term "large" refers not only to the size of the datasets used for training but also to the complexity of the models themselves. LLMs are built using layers of artificial neurons arranged in sophisticated architectures, enabling them to capture intricate patterns in data. These models are designed to process sequences of words (or tokens) and generate outputs that align with the context, making them highly adaptable and versatile.

The Role of Training Data

The training process for LLMs involves exposing the model to an extensive corpus of text data, often sourced from books, websites, articles, and other publicly available materials. This diverse dataset allows the model to acquire a broad understanding of language, encompassing grammar, syntax, semantics, and even cultural references.

During training, LLMs use algorithms to predict the next word in a sequence based on the preceding words. This task, known as "language modeling," helps the model learn the probabilities of word combinations, enabling it to generate coherent and contextually appropriate text. The more extensive and diverse the training data, the better the model's ability to generalize across different topics and contexts.

However, the reliance on large datasets also introduces challenges, such as the potential for biases or inaccuracies present in the data to be reflected in the model's outputs. Addressing these issues requires careful curation of training datasets and post-training techniques to align the model's behavior with ethical standards.

How Do LLMs Work?

To understand how LLMs function, it's essential to explore their underlying architecture and operational principles. Most modern LLMs are based on transformer architectures, which have become the gold standard for NLP tasks due to their efficiency and scalability.

1. Tokenization: The First Step

Before processing text, LLMs convert it into a numerical format that can be interpreted by the model. This process, called tokenization, involves breaking down text into smaller units known as tokens. Tokens can represent individual words, subwords, or even characters, depending on the tokenization scheme.

For example, the sentence "Large Language Models are fascinating" might be tokenized into the following sequence: ["Large," "Language," "Models," "are," "fascinating"]. Each token is then mapped to a unique numerical representation, such as an embedding vector, which serves as the input to the model.

2. Embeddings: Representing Words in High Dimensions

Once text is tokenized, each token is transformed into an embedding—a dense vector representation in a high-dimensional space. These embeddings capture semantic relationships between words, allowing the model to understand context and meaning. For instance, the words "king" and "queen" might have similar embeddings, reflecting their semantic similarity.

3. The Transformer Architecture

Transformers are the backbone of modern LLMs, enabling them to process and generate language effectively. The architecture consists of multiple layers of attention mechanisms and feedforward neural networks. The key components of transformers include:

- **Self-Attention Mechanism:** This mechanism allows the model to focus on different parts of the input sequence, assigning varying degrees of importance to each token. For example, in the sentence "The cat sat on the mat," the word "mat" may have a strong connection to "on" and "sat," which helps the model understand the relationships between words.

- **Positional Encoding:** Since transformers do not inherently understand the order of tokens, positional encoding is used to inject information about token positions into the embeddings.

- **Feedforward Layers:** These layers process the output of the attention mechanism, introducing non-linearity and enabling the model to capture complex patterns.

4. Training: Learning from Data

Training an LLM involves optimizing its parameters to minimize the difference between its predicted outputs and the actual data. This process is guided by a loss function, which quantifies the model's errors. The most common approach is supervised pretraining, where the model learns to predict the next token in a sequence based on context.

Once pretrained, LLMs can undergo fine-tuning—a process where they are further trained on domain-specific data to specialize in particular tasks. For instance, a general-purpose LLM might be fine-tuned on legal documents to assist in contract review or on medical texts to support clinical decision-making.

5. Inference: Generating Outputs

Inference refers to the process of using a trained LLM to generate outputs. When given an input prompt, the model processes it through its layers to produce a sequence of tokens as the output. This process involves sampling from the model's probability distribution over possible tokens, guided by parameters like temperature (which controls randomness) and top-k sampling (which limits token selection to the most probable options).

For example, if prompted with "Write a poem about the ocean," the model generates text by predicting one token at a time until it completes a coherent output, such as:

The ocean whispers tales of old,
Beneath the waves, its secrets unfold.

The Versatility of LLMs

The versatility of LLMs stems from their ability to perform a wide array of tasks without extensive task-specific training. This capability, known as few-shot or zero-shot learning, allows LLMs to generalize from minimal examples or even infer solutions without prior exposure to a task.

For instance:

- **Few-Shot Learning:** Given a prompt with a few examples, such as "Translate the following: Bonjour → Hello, Merci → Thank you," the model can infer how to translate new phrases.
- **Zero-Shot Learning:** When asked to generate a summary for an article without explicit examples, the model leverages its pretraining to produce a concise summary.

This adaptability has made LLMs invaluable across industries, powering applications in customer service, content creation, education, and more.

Challenges and Limitations

Despite their remarkable capabilities, LLMs are not without limitations. Common challenges include:

- **Bias in Outputs:** Since LLMs learn from vast datasets that may contain biased or inaccurate information, they can inadvertently produce biased outputs.
- **Resource Intensity:** Training and deploying LLMs require substantial computational resources, making them inaccessible to smaller organizations.
- **Lack of True Understanding:** While LLMs excel at pattern recognition, they lack genuine comprehension or reasoning abilities, which can lead to errors in complex or nuanced scenarios.
- **Ethical Concerns:** The potential misuse of LLMs for generating misinformation or deepfake content raises ethical questions about their deployment.

Conclusion

Large Language Models represent a paradigm shift in artificial intelligence, enabling machines to process and generate human language with unparalleled accuracy and flexibility. By leveraging transformer architectures, massive datasets, and advanced training techniques, LLMs have unlocked new possibilities across industries and applications. While challenges remain, ongoing advancements in architecture, training methods, and ethical considerations continue to push the boundaries of what LLMs can achieve. Understanding how LLMs work is the first step in harnessing their transformative potential and contributing to the next wave of AI innovation.

LLM Architecture: Encoders, Decoders, and Attention Mechanisms

The architecture of Large Language Models (LLMs) lies at the heart of their groundbreaking capabilities. By understanding the underlying mechanisms—encoders, decoders, and attention mechanisms—we can better appreciate how these models process and generate human-like language with remarkable accuracy and coherence. This chapter explores the core architectural components of LLMs, shedding light on their functionality and the innovations that have propelled them to the forefront of artificial intelligence.

The Transformer: A Revolution in AI

Modern LLMs are built on the transformer architecture, introduced in the seminal paper "Attention Is All You Need" by Vaswani et al. in 2017. Transformers have replaced older architectures like recurrent neural networks (RNNs) and long short-term memory (LSTM) networks due to their ability to process sequences of text more efficiently and effectively. The key innovation in transformers is the attention mechanism, which allows models to focus on relevant parts of the input while processing sequences in parallel.

Transformers consist of two primary components: the encoder and the decoder. While some models use only the encoder (e.g., BERT) or only the decoder (e.g., GPT), others integrate both components for more comprehensive capabilities (e.g., T5).

Encoders: Understanding the Input

The encoder's role in a transformer is to process and encode the input text into a series of dense vector representations. These representations capture the meaning and relationships between words, enabling the model to understand the context of the input.

Structure of the Encoder

An encoder typically consists of multiple identical layers, each containing two main sub-components:

1. **Self-Attention Mechanism:** This mechanism allows the model to determine which parts of the input are most relevant to each token. By calculating attention scores, the encoder assigns weights to different tokens based on their relationships, enabling it to focus on the most pertinent information. For instance, in the sentence "The cat sat on the mat," the word "mat" is strongly related to "sat" and "on," and the self-attention mechanism captures these dependencies.

2. **Feedforward Neural Network:** After the self-attention mechanism, the token representations are passed through a feedforward neural network. This component introduces non-linearity, allowing the model to capture complex patterns and relationships within the data.

Each encoder layer also includes residual connections and layer normalization to stabilize training and improve performance.

Encoder-Only Models

Some LLMs, such as BERT (Bidirectional Encoder Representations from Transformers), use only the encoder stack. These models are designed for tasks that require understanding and analyzing input text, such as text classification, sentiment analysis, and question answering. By leveraging bidirectional self-attention, encoder-only models can consider both the left and right context of each token, providing a holistic understanding of the input.

Decoders: Generating the Output

While encoders focus on understanding the input, decoders are responsible for generating output sequences, such as text completions, translations, or responses. Decoders process the input representations (from the encoder or the initial embedding) and produce tokens one at a time until the desired output is complete.

Structure of the Decoder

Like encoders, decoders consist of multiple identical layers. However, they include additional mechanisms to handle both input and previously generated tokens:

1. **Self-Attention Mechanism:** This component operates similarly to the encoder's self-attention but is masked to ensure that the model cannot "look ahead" at future tokens during generation. This causal masking ensures that the output sequence is generated in a left-to-right manner.

2. **Encoder-Decoder Attention Mechanism:** Unique to decoders, this mechanism allows the decoder to focus on the encoder's output representations while generating each token. By attending to relevant parts of the input, the decoder can produce contextually appropriate and coherent outputs.

3. **Feedforward Neural Network:** As in the encoder, this component processes the attention outputs to capture complex patterns and relationships.

Decoder-Only Models

Models like GPT (Generative Pre-trained Transformer) use only the decoder stack. These models are optimized for generative tasks, including text completion, creative writing, and chatbot responses. By training on large corpora of text, decoder-only models learn to predict the next token in a sequence based on the context provided by preceding tokens.

Attention Mechanisms: The Key to Context

The attention mechanism is the cornerstone of the transformer architecture, enabling models to capture relationships between tokens and focus on relevant information. Unlike older architectures that processed sequences sequentially, attention allows transformers to process entire sequences in parallel, significantly improving efficiency and scalability.

How Attention Works

At a high level, the attention mechanism computes a weighted sum of the input tokens, where the weights represent the importance of each token relative to others. This process involves three key components:

1. **Query (Q):** Represents the token for which the attention is being calculated.

2. **Key (K):** Represents the context or reference tokens.

3. **Value (V):** Represents the information associated with each token.

The attention score for each token pair is computed as the dot product of the query and key vectors, scaled by the square root of the vector dimension. These scores are then normalized using a softmax function to produce attention weights, which are applied to the value vectors to generate the final output.

Self-Attention vs. Cross-Attention

- **Self-Attention:** Used within the encoder and decoder layers, self-attention enables tokens to focus on other tokens within the same sequence. This mechanism is crucial for capturing dependencies and relationships across the input or output sequence.
- **Cross-Attention:** Used in encoder-decoder models, cross-attention allows the decoder to focus on the encoder's output representations. This mechanism ensures that the generated text is closely aligned with the input context, as seen in tasks like translation or summarization.

Multi-Head Attention

To enhance the model's ability to capture diverse relationships, transformers employ multi-head attention. Instead of computing a single set of attention scores, the model uses multiple attention heads, each with its own query, key, and value projections. These heads operate in parallel, capturing different aspects of the input sequence and improving the model's expressiveness.

The outputs of all attention heads are concatenated and passed through a linear layer to produce the final attention output.

Combining Encoders, Decoders, and Attention

When encoders, decoders, and attention mechanisms work in harmony, they enable transformers to excel at a wide range of NLP tasks. For example:

- In machine translation, the encoder processes the source text (e.g., English) and generates a context-aware representation, which the decoder uses to produce the target text (e.g., French).
- In text summarization, the encoder captures the key ideas from a long document, while the decoder generates a concise summary.
- In conversational AI, decoder-only models like GPT generate contextually relevant and coherent responses based on user input.

Advances and Variations in Architecture

Over time, researchers have developed variations of the transformer architecture to address specific challenges and improve performance:

- **Bidirectional Transformers:** Models like BERT use bidirectional self-attention to capture context from both directions, enhancing their understanding of input text.
- **Autoregressive Transformers:** Models like GPT use unidirectional attention for generative tasks, ensuring outputs are produced sequentially.
- **Encoder-Decoder Models:** Models like T5 and BART combine encoders and decoders for tasks that require both understanding and generation.
- **Sparse Attention:** To reduce computational costs, some models use sparse attention mechanisms that focus only on a subset of tokens, improving efficiency without sacrificing performance.

Conclusion

The architecture of LLMs—rooted in encoders, decoders, and attention mechanisms—has revolutionized natural language processing by enabling models to process and generate human language with unprecedented accuracy and versatility. By leveraging the power of transformers, these models have unlocked new possibilities in fields ranging from translation and summarization to creative writing and conversational AI. As researchers continue to refine and innovate upon these architectures, the potential of LLMs to transform industries and enhance human-machine interaction will only grow.

Key Players: GPT, Llama, Falcon, and Beyond

In the dynamic world of artificial intelligence (AI), Large Language Models (LLMs) are at the forefront of technological innovation. Among these, several key players have emerged, each contributing unique capabilities and architectural advancements that push the boundaries of natural language processing (NLP). This chapter delves into the prominent LLMs shaping the industry today—GPT, Llama, Falcon, and beyond—exploring their distinguishing features, applications, and impact on the AI landscape.

GPT: The Pioneer of Generative Language Models

The Generative Pre-trained Transformer (GPT) series, developed by OpenAI, stands as one of the most influential contributions to the field of AI. GPT models are autoregressive language models that generate text by predicting the next word in a sequence, based on the context provided by preceding words. This approach, combined with transformer-based architecture, has made GPT a cornerstone in the development of generative AI.

Evolution of GPT

- **GPT-1:** Released in 2018, GPT-1 introduced the concept of pretraining on large datasets followed by fine-tuning for specific tasks. Despite its modest size compared to today's models, it demonstrated the potential of transformer-based architectures.

- **GPT-2:** GPT-2, launched in 2019, marked a significant leap in model size and performance. With 1.5 billion parameters, it showcased impressive text generation capabilities, sparking public fascination with AI's creative potential.

- **GPT-3:** Released in 2020, GPT-3 expanded the parameter count to 175 billion, offering unparalleled text generation, summarization, translation, and more. Its ability to perform tasks with minimal examples, known as few-shot and zero-shot learning, revolutionized how LLMs are applied across industries.

- **GPT-4:** Building on its predecessors, GPT-4 introduced improved multimodal capabilities, allowing the model to process and generate text, images, and other data types. This advance made GPT-4 a versatile tool for both professional and creative applications.

Applications of GPT

GPT models are widely used in chatbots, virtual assistants, content generation, programming support, and educational tools. Their ability to handle diverse tasks has made them a cornerstone for businesses seeking to leverage AI-driven solutions.

Llama: Democratizing Access to LLMs

Meta (formerly Facebook) introduced Llama (Large Language Model Meta AI) as a response to the growing demand for accessible and efficient LLMs. Llama's key differentiator lies in its emphasis on smaller, high-performing models that are computationally efficient and open to researchers.

Llama's Design Philosophy

Llama was designed to address two critical challenges in the LLM space:

1. **Accessibility:** Unlike proprietary models like GPT, Llama focuses on democratizing AI research by making its architecture and weights available to researchers and developers.

2. **Efficiency:** By optimizing model size without sacrificing performance, Llama achieves competitive results using fewer computational resources.

Applications of Llama

Llama is particularly popular in academic and research settings, where accessibility and adaptability are paramount. Its open nature allows researchers to experiment, innovate, and contribute to advancing the field of AI.

Falcon: Optimized for Industrial Applications

Falcon, developed by the Technology Innovation Institute, represents another significant player in the LLM ecosystem. Focused on industrial applications, Falcon is known for its high efficiency and performance, making it a preferred choice for enterprises with large-scale AI requirements.

Key Features of Falcon

- **Scalability:** Falcon models are designed to handle extensive datasets and perform well across diverse tasks, from data analysis to automated content creation.

- **Adaptability:** By offering pre-trained models that can be fine-tuned for specific use cases, Falcon ensures that businesses can customize AI solutions to their unique needs.

- **Integration:** Falcon integrates seamlessly with existing enterprise systems, providing a practical and scalable solution for organizations.

Applications of Falcon

Falcon's industrial focus makes it an ideal choice for sectors such as finance, healthcare, and logistics. Its ability to process large volumes of data efficiently and provide actionable insights has made it a key player in enterprise-level AI deployments.

Beyond GPT, Llama, and Falcon: Emerging Contenders

While GPT, Llama, and Falcon dominate much of the LLM conversation, several other models are contributing to the field's rapid evolution. These emerging contenders bring unique innovations and capabilities, addressing specific challenges and broadening the scope of what LLMs can achieve.

BERT: Focused on Understanding

Bidirectional Encoder Representations from Transformers (BERT), developed by Google, is a trailblazer in bidirectional language understanding. Unlike autoregressive models like GPT, BERT processes entire sequences bidirectionally, enabling it to grasp context from both preceding and succeeding words.

- **Applications:** BERT excels in tasks like sentiment analysis, question answering, and natural language inference.
- **Impact:** BERT's introduction revolutionized NLP benchmarks, setting a new standard for understanding-based tasks.

T5: A Unified Framework for NLP

The Text-to-Text Transfer Transformer (T5) by Google simplifies NLP tasks by framing them all as text-to-text problems. This unified approach allows T5 to perform a wide range of tasks, from translation to summarization, using a consistent framework.

- **Applications:** T5 is widely used in multi-task learning and applications requiring high adaptability.
- **Impact:** T5's flexibility and performance have made it a favorite among researchers and practitioners.

Claude: A New Approach to Alignment

Developed by Anthropic, Claude focuses on aligning AI behavior with human values. By emphasizing safety and ethical considerations, Claude represents a shift toward responsible AI development.

- **Applications:** Claude is designed for use in conversational AI, content moderation, and applications requiring high alignment with human intent.
- **Impact:** By prioritizing safety and ethics, Claude sets a benchmark for the responsible deployment of LLMs.

Bloom: Open and Collaborative

Bloom is a multilingual LLM developed by a collaboration of researchers and organizations worldwide. It is designed to support diverse languages and foster open collaboration in AI research.

- **Applications:** Bloom is used for multilingual NLP tasks, cultural preservation, and cross-lingual research.
- **Impact:** Bloom's emphasis on inclusivity and openness has expanded the reach of LLMs to underrepresented languages and communities.

Comparative Insights: Choosing the Right Model

Each LLM brings unique strengths and trade-offs, making the choice of model dependent on the specific use case:

- **For Generative Tasks:** GPT remains the gold standard for creative and conversational applications, offering unparalleled versatility and scale.
- **For Research and Accessibility:** Llama's open architecture makes it ideal for academic exploration and smaller-scale applications.
- **For Industrial Efficiency:** Falcon's scalability and integration capabilities cater to enterprise-level demands.

- **For Contextual Understanding:** BERT's bidirectional processing excels in tasks requiring deep comprehension of text.
- **For Unified NLP Tasks:** T5's text-to-text framework simplifies multi-task learning and adaptation.
- **For Ethical AI:** Claude's focus on alignment ensures safer and more responsible AI deployments.
- **For Multilingual Applications:** Bloom's multilingual design addresses the needs of diverse linguistic communities.

Future Directions and Emerging Trends

The rapid pace of innovation in the LLM space suggests a future where these models become even more integrated into daily life and industrial processes. Key trends to watch include:

- **Multimodal Models:** The integration of text, image, and audio data will enable more holistic AI applications, as seen in models like GPT-4.
- **Domain-Specific LLMs:** Tailored models for specific industries, such as healthcare and law, will enhance precision and relevance.
- **Energy Efficiency:** As sustainability becomes a priority, researchers are focusing on developing LLMs that require less computational power.
- **Ethical AI:** Ongoing efforts to align LLMs with human values will shape how these models are deployed responsibly.

Conclusion

The landscape of Large Language Models is rich and diverse, with key players like GPT, Llama, Falcon, and others driving advancements across industries. Each model brings unique capabilities and innovations, addressing specific challenges and expanding the possibilities of what AI can achieve. By understanding the strengths and applications of these models, we can harness their potential to create transformative solutions and shape the future of human-AI collaboration.

Chapter 4: Building Blocks of LLM Applications

The Role of Data: Embeddings, Tokenization, and Context

Data is the cornerstone of every Large Language Model (LLM). Its ability to understand, generate, and interact with human language hinges on how effectively it processes and utilizes data. Central to this process are three foundational concepts: embeddings, tokenization, and context. These elements enable LLMs to interpret raw text, capture nuanced relationships, and generate coherent responses. This chapter delves into the role of these building blocks, exploring their significance, mechanics, and impact on the performance of LLM applications.

Tokenization: Breaking Down Language

Tokenization is the first step in processing language data for LLMs. It involves breaking down raw text into smaller, manageable units called tokens. These tokens can represent words, subwords, or even individual characters, depending on the tokenization strategy used.

Types of Tokenization

1. **Word-Level Tokenization:** This method treats each word in a text as a single token. For example, the sentence "The cat sat on the mat" would be tokenized as: ["The," "cat," "sat," "on," "the," "mat"]. While straightforward, this approach struggles with handling out-of-vocabulary words, like rare or misspelled terms.

2. **Subword-Level Tokenization:** Subword tokenization, used in models like BERT and GPT, breaks words into smaller units, such as prefixes, suffixes, or roots. For instance, the word "unbelievable" might be tokenized as ["un," "believ," "able"]. This approach balances vocabulary size and adaptability, allowing models to handle novel words more effectively.

3. **Character-Level Tokenization:** In this approach, every character is treated as a token. For example, "at" would be tokenized as ["a," "t"]. While highly adaptable, character-level tokenization can result in longer sequences, increasing computational complexity.

Importance of Tokenization

Tokenization is critical because it transforms raw text into a format that LLMs can process. The choice of tokenization strategy impacts the model's efficiency, performance, and ability to generalize. For example, subword tokenization strikes a balance between vocabulary size and handling rare words, making it a popular choice in modern LLMs.

Embeddings: Representing Text in High Dimensions

Once text is tokenized, the next step is to convert tokens into numerical representations, known as embeddings. These embeddings are dense vectors in high-dimensional space, designed to capture the semantic meaning of the tokens.

How Embeddings Work

Embeddings are generated using a technique called word vectorization. Each token is mapped to a vector, where the dimensions of the vector correspond to specific features of the word's meaning or usage. For example, embeddings for "king" and "queen" might be close in space, reflecting their semantic similarity, while "king" and "car" would be farther apart.

Types of Embedding Models

1. **Word2Vec:** Introduced in 2013, Word2Vec generates word embeddings by training a shallow neural network to predict surrounding words (context) for a given word. It uses two approaches:

    o **Skip-Gram:** Predicts context words based on a target word.

    o **Continuous Bag of Words (CBOW):** Predicts a target word based on surrounding context words.

2. **GloVe (Global Vectors for Word Representation):** GloVe creates embeddings by analyzing word co-occurrence in a corpus. It captures global statistical information about word relationships, providing robust embeddings for large datasets.

3. **Contextual Embeddings (e.g., BERT):** Unlike static embeddings like Word2Vec and GloVe, contextual embeddings generate word vectors that vary depending on the surrounding context. For example, the word "bank" in "sit by the bank" and "open a bank account" would have different embeddings, reflecting their distinct meanings.

Applications of Embeddings

Embeddings are essential for tasks like:

- **Semantic Search:** Finding documents or passages that are semantically similar to a query.
- **Text Classification:** Assigning categories to text based on its content.
- **Translation:** Mapping words or phrases between languages while preserving meaning.

By representing language in a high-dimensional space, embeddings allow LLMs to understand relationships, similarities, and differences between words, sentences, and documents.

Context: Capturing Relationships and Meaning

Context is the backbone of language understanding. It provides the necessary information for interpreting the meaning of words and sentences. LLMs rely on context to disambiguate words, resolve pronouns, and generate coherent text.

How Context is Captured

Modern LLMs use mechanisms like attention to capture context effectively. The self-attention mechanism in transformer architectures allows the model to assign weights to different tokens based on their relevance to the current token.

For instance, in the sentence "The cat sat on the mat because it was warm," the word "it" refers to "mat." Through attention mechanisms, the model learns this relationship, enabling it to generate accurate and contextually appropriate responses.

Contextual Relationships in Sentences

1. **Syntactic Relationships:** These involve the grammatical structure of a sentence, such as subject-verb-object relationships. For example, in "The dog chased the ball," the model recognizes "dog" as the subject, "chased" as the verb, and "ball" as the object.

2. **Semantic Relationships:** These involve the meaning of words and phrases. For instance, the words "hot" and "cold" are antonyms, while "summer" and "vacation" are often related conceptually.

3. **Coreference Resolution:** This refers to identifying when different words or phrases refer to the same entity. For example, in "Alice picked up her book and started reading it," the model understands that "it" refers to "book."

Role of Context in Generation Tasks

In generative tasks, context is vital for producing coherent and relevant text. For example:

- **Summarization:** The model uses the context of an entire document to generate a concise summary.

- **Dialogue Systems:** In conversations, the model relies on prior exchanges to generate contextually appropriate responses.

- **Creative Writing:** Context ensures that generated stories or poems maintain logical consistency and flow.

Challenges in Data Processing

While tokenization, embeddings, and context are powerful tools, they also present challenges:

1. **Ambiguity in Language:** Words often have multiple meanings, which can confuse models without sufficient context. For example, "bank" could mean a financial institution or the side of a river.

2. **Long-Range Dependencies:** Capturing relationships between distant tokens in a sequence can be challenging, particularly for older architectures. Transformers address this issue with self-attention but can still struggle with extremely long texts.

3. **Bias in Data:** The quality and diversity of training data significantly impact model performance. Biased or unrepresentative data can lead to biased or inaccurate outputs.

4. **Scalability:** Processing massive datasets and generating embeddings for large corpora require substantial computational resources, posing challenges for smaller organizations.

Advances in Data Processing for LLMs

To overcome these challenges, researchers have introduced several innovations:

- **Dynamic Tokenization:** Techniques like SentencePiece and Byte-Pair Encoding (BPE) dynamically create token vocabularies, improving adaptability to diverse languages and contexts.

- **Efficient Attention Mechanisms:** Advances like sparse attention and longformer architectures enhance the ability to process long sequences efficiently.

- **Denoising Objectives:** Models like BART use denoising tasks during training to improve robustness and context understanding.

Conclusion

The role of data in LLMs—from tokenization and embeddings to context—is foundational to their ability to process and generate human-like language. Tokenization breaks down text into manageable units, embeddings translate those units into meaningful numerical representations, and context ties it all together, enabling coherent and accurate outputs. By mastering these building blocks, we can harness the full potential of LLMs, creating applications that revolutionize industries and enhance human-AI interaction.

Exploring Pretrained Models vs. Building from Scratch

The development of Large Language Models (LLMs) has opened a pivotal debate in artificial intelligence (AI): should you rely on pretrained models or build your own LLM from scratch? Each approach offers distinct advantages and challenges, and the decision ultimately hinges on your objectives, resources, and expertise. This chapter delves into the key differences between these two strategies, exploring their technical, financial, and operational implications.

Pretrained Models: Leveraging Existing Resources

Pretrained models are LLMs that have already undergone extensive training on large datasets, often comprising billions of parameters and terabytes of data. They are designed to perform a wide range of natural language processing (NLP) tasks out of the box or with minimal customization.

Advantages of Pretrained Models

1. **Cost Efficiency:** Training an LLM from scratch requires substantial computational resources and access to vast datasets. Pretrained models, on the other hand, allow organizations to bypass these upfront costs. For example, accessing GPT-4 or Llama 2 via APIs or open-source platforms eliminates the need for expensive infrastructure.

2. **Time Savings:** Training a model from scratch can take weeks or months, depending on its size and complexity. Pretrained models are ready to use almost immediately, significantly reducing time-to-market for AI solutions.

3. **Versatility:** Pretrained models are trained on diverse datasets, enabling them to generalize across multiple domains. This versatility makes them suitable for a wide range of tasks, including text generation, summarization, translation, and more.

4. **Ease of Customization:** Fine-tuning a pretrained model on domain-specific data is often straightforward. For instance, a medical organization can fine-tune a general-purpose LLM on healthcare data to create an AI system tailored to medical diagnoses and documentation.

5. **Community Support and Documentation:** Popular pretrained models, such as OpenAI's GPT series or Hugging Face's BERT implementations, are supported by extensive documentation, active developer communities, and prebuilt libraries. These resources simplify integration and troubleshooting.

Challenges of Pretrained Models

1. **Limited Customization:** While pretrained models can be fine-tuned, their architecture and core functionalities are fixed. This limitation can be a drawback for organizations with unique requirements that demand extensive customization.

2. **Dependence on External Providers:** Using proprietary pretrained models often entails reliance on third-party providers, raising concerns about data privacy, compliance, and long-term accessibility.

3. **Ethical and Bias Concerns:** Pretrained models inherit biases present in their training data. Addressing these biases may require additional layers of filtering or fine-tuning, which can be complex and resource-intensive.

4. **Scalability Costs:** While pretrained models save on initial training costs, their operational expenses can be significant, especially when deployed at scale. Cloud usage fees for APIs or hosting large models locally can add up quickly.

Building Models from Scratch: Tailored Solutions

Building an LLM from scratch involves designing its architecture, curating datasets, and training the model from the ground up. While resource-intensive, this approach offers unparalleled control and customization.

Advantages of Building from Scratch

1. **Full Customization:** Building a model from scratch allows developers to tailor every aspect of the architecture, training process, and data pipeline to meet specific requirements. For example, a legal firm could create an LLM optimized for parsing legal documents with unparalleled accuracy.

2. **Proprietary Control:** Organizations that develop their own models retain full ownership of the intellectual property (IP), eliminating dependency on external vendors. This independence is critical for industries with stringent data privacy or regulatory requirements.

3. **Addressing Domain-Specific Needs:** Training a model on highly specialized data ensures optimal performance in niche applications. For example, a model trained exclusively on scientific research papers may outperform general-purpose LLMs in summarizing research findings.

4. **Ethical and Transparent Development:** Building a model from scratch allows organizations to curate their datasets carefully, ensuring transparency and reducing inherent biases. This control is vital for creating ethical AI systems.

Challenges of Building from Scratch

1. **Resource Requirements:** Training an LLM from scratch demands extensive computational power, typically involving high-performance GPUs or TPUs, and access to vast amounts of labeled data. Organizations without these resources may struggle to achieve competitive results.

2. **Expertise and Development Time:** Designing, training, and optimizing a model from scratch requires significant technical expertise and time. Organizations must invest in skilled data scientists, machine learning engineers, and domain experts.

3. **High Initial Costs:** The upfront costs of developing a model from scratch—including infrastructure, talent acquisition, and data collection—can be prohibitively high for small and medium-sized enterprises.

4. **Risk of Underperformance:** Without access to the scale and diversity of data used in pretrained models, custom-built models may struggle to match their performance, especially in general-purpose tasks.

Key Considerations for Choosing Between Pretrained Models and Building from Scratch

Project Objectives

- If your project requires general NLP capabilities, pretrained models are typically sufficient and cost-effective.
- For projects with unique requirements, such as specialized language understanding or integration with proprietary systems, building a custom model may be worth the investment.

Budget and Resources

- Pretrained models are ideal for organizations with limited budgets or computational resources.
- Organizations with substantial funding and technical expertise can consider building from scratch to achieve tailored solutions.

Time-to-Market

- Pretrained models significantly reduce development timelines, making them suitable for projects with tight deadlines.
- Building a model from scratch requires long development cycles, which may not align with urgent business needs.

Ethical and Regulatory Requirements

- Industries with strict regulatory requirements may benefit from the transparency and control offered by custom-built models.
- Pretrained models can be fine-tuned to meet compliance standards, but this process may involve additional effort.

Long-Term Goals

- Pretrained models offer scalability and ease of integration for evolving projects.
- Custom models provide a foundation for long-term innovation, particularly in fields where proprietary technology is a competitive advantage.

Hybrid Approaches: The Best of Both Worlds

Many organizations adopt a hybrid approach, leveraging pretrained models as a foundation while incorporating custom training to meet specific needs. For instance:

1. **Fine-Tuning Pretrained Models:** By retraining a pretrained model on domain-specific data, organizations can achieve a balance between customization and cost-efficiency. For example, fine-tuning GPT-4 on legal texts creates a specialized model for legal document analysis.

2. **Transfer Learning:** Transfer learning involves using a pretrained model's weights as a starting point and continuing training on a different dataset. This approach reduces training time and resource requirements while retaining the benefits of customization.

3. **Adapter Modules:** Adapter modules are lightweight, task-specific layers added to a pretrained model. They allow for efficient customization without retraining the entire model, making them a popular choice for resource-constrained projects.

Future Trends in Pretrained and Custom Models

The debate between pretrained models and building from scratch is evolving as AI technology advances. Key trends to watch include:

- **Smaller, More Efficient Models:** Efforts to create smaller, high-performing models, such as Meta's Llama, reduce the barriers to building custom models.

- **Open-Source Ecosystems:** Open-source initiatives like Hugging Face are democratizing access to pretrained models and tools, enabling greater innovation in custom development.

- **Ethical AI Development:** Increasing emphasis on transparency and accountability is driving organizations to invest in curated datasets and ethical model training practices.

- **Specialized Architectures:** Advances in domain-specific architectures will blur the lines between pretrained and custom models, offering highly optimized solutions for niche applications.

Conclusion

The choice between pretrained models and building from scratch is not a binary decision but a spectrum of possibilities. Pretrained models excel in accessibility, cost-efficiency, and versatility, making them the go-to option for many organizations. Conversely, building from scratch offers unparalleled control, customization, and proprietary ownership, appealing to industries with unique requirements. By carefully evaluating project objectives, resources, and long-term goals, organizations can make informed decisions that align with their needs, leveraging the best of both worlds to unlock the full potential of LLMs.

Ethical Considerations and Responsible AI

The development and deployment of Large Language Models (LLMs) have transformed industries, empowered individuals, and reshaped how society interacts with artificial intelligence. However, the remarkable capabilities of these systems also come with significant ethical responsibilities. As LLMs become increasingly integrated into applications ranging from conversational agents to decision-support systems, ethical considerations must be at the forefront of their design, deployment, and governance. This chapter explores the critical ethical challenges associated with LLMs, the principles of responsible AI, and strategies for mitigating potential harms.

Bias and Fairness in LLMs

One of the most pressing ethical issues with LLMs is their susceptibility to bias. These models are trained on vast datasets sourced from the internet, books, and other publicly available materials, which often reflect societal biases and stereotypes. As a result, LLMs can inadvertently perpetuate or even amplify these biases in their outputs.

Sources of Bias

1. **Training Data Bias:** The data used to train LLMs may overrepresent certain demographics, viewpoints, or cultural norms while underrepresenting others. For example, if a dataset contains predominantly

Western perspectives, the model may produce outputs that marginalize non-Western cultures or viewpoints.

2. **Algorithmic Bias:** Even if the data itself is balanced, the algorithms used to train LLMs may introduce bias. Certain optimization techniques or architectural choices can inadvertently prioritize one type of content over another.

3. **User Interaction Bias:** The way users interact with LLMs can reinforce biases. For instance, if users frequently prompt a model with biased queries, the model may adjust its responses to align with those biases.

Mitigating Bias

Addressing bias requires a multi-faceted approach:

- **Dataset Curation:** Carefully curating diverse and representative datasets can help mitigate bias at its source.

- **Bias Audits:** Regularly auditing models for biased behavior ensures that issues are identified and addressed promptly.

- **Fine-Tuning:** Retraining models on balanced datasets or applying post-processing techniques can reduce biased outputs.

- **Transparency:** Clearly documenting the limitations and potential biases of a model helps users understand its context and constraints.

Misinformation and Hallucination

Another significant ethical concern with LLMs is their tendency to generate misinformation or hallucinations—outputs that are factually incorrect or entirely fabricated. While LLMs are highly adept at generating coherent and convincing text, they lack an inherent understanding of truth or context.

Risks of Misinformation

1. **Public Trust:** Misinformation generated by LLMs can erode public trust in AI systems, particularly if these models are used in critical domains such as healthcare, education, or governance.

2. **Amplification of Falsehoods:** If unchecked, LLMs can amplify conspiracy theories, pseudoscience, or other harmful narratives, spreading them to a wider audience.

3. **Legal and Reputational Risks:** Organizations deploying LLMs may face legal or reputational consequences if their systems disseminate false or misleading information.

Mitigating Misinformation

- **Fact-Checking:** Incorporating fact-checking mechanisms into LLM pipelines ensures that outputs are cross-referenced against reliable sources.

- **Human Oversight:** In high-stakes applications, human reviewers should validate critical outputs before they are published or acted upon.

- **Reinforcement Learning with Human Feedback (RLHF):** Training models to prioritize factual accuracy using human-curated datasets can reduce hallucination rates.

Privacy and Data Security

The training and deployment of LLMs often involve large-scale data collection, raising significant privacy and security concerns. Users interacting with LLMs may unknowingly disclose sensitive information, while the training data itself may contain private or proprietary content.

Privacy Risks

1. **Data Leakage:** During training, models may inadvertently memorize specific data points, such as credit card numbers or personal identifiers, and reproduce them in outputs.
2. **User Data Exploitation:** Interactive LLMs that collect user queries can become repositories of sensitive information, making them attractive targets for malicious actors.
3. **Lack of Transparency:** Users may be unaware of how their interactions with LLMs are stored, processed, or shared.

Ensuring Privacy

- **Anonymization:** Removing personally identifiable information from training datasets reduces the risk of data leakage.
- **Secure Storage:** Encrypting user data and implementing robust access controls ensures that sensitive information is protected.
- **Transparency Policies:** Clearly communicating how user data is handled builds trust and fosters responsible use.
- **Differential Privacy:** Techniques like differential privacy can be used during training to prevent models from memorizing sensitive data.

Accountability and Transparency

As LLMs are increasingly deployed in decision-making processes, questions of accountability and transparency become critical. Users and stakeholders must understand how models make decisions and who is responsible for their outcomes.

Challenges to Accountability

1. **Opacity:** The complex architectures of LLMs make them difficult to interpret, creating a "black box" effect.
2. **Shared Responsibility:** In collaborative ecosystems involving model developers, data providers, and end-users, determining accountability can be challenging.
3. **Unintended Consequences:** Models may produce unexpected outputs that lead to harmful outcomes, raising questions about liability.

Promoting Transparency

- **Explainability Tools:** Developing tools to explain model outputs and decision pathways helps demystify LLM behavior.
- **Clear Documentation:** Comprehensive documentation of a model's training process, datasets, and limitations fosters transparency.
- **Ethical AI Frameworks:** Adopting established ethical AI frameworks ensures that accountability is embedded in the development lifecycle.

Deployment in High-Stakes Domains

The deployment of LLMs in critical sectors such as healthcare, law, and education amplifies the ethical stakes. In these domains, errors or biases can have profound consequences, affecting lives and livelihoods.

Healthcare

- **Opportunities:** LLMs can assist in diagnosing diseases, drafting medical reports, and providing patient education.
- **Risks:** Incorrect outputs or misinterpretations can lead to harmful medical decisions.
- **Best Practices:** Ensuring human oversight and integrating domain-specific expertise are essential for ethical deployment.

Law

- **Opportunities:** LLMs can streamline legal research, draft contracts, and simplify complex legal language.
- **Risks:** Misinterpretation of legal precedents or biased outputs can result in unfair outcomes.
- **Best Practices:** Models should be rigorously tested on legal datasets, with trained professionals validating their outputs.

Education

- **Opportunities:** LLMs can provide personalized learning experiences, generate educational content, and support student engagement.
- **Risks:** Over-reliance on AI-generated content may undermine critical thinking or propagate inaccuracies.
- **Best Practices:** AI tools should complement, not replace, traditional educational methods.

Ethical Guidelines and Governance

To navigate these challenges, ethical guidelines and governance frameworks are essential. These principles provide a roadmap for responsible AI development and deployment.

Core Principles of Ethical AI

1. **Fairness:** Ensure that AI systems treat all users equitably, avoiding discrimination or bias.

2. **Transparency:** Make AI processes and decision-making pathways understandable to users and stakeholders.
3. **Accountability:** Establish clear lines of responsibility for AI outcomes, ensuring that developers and deployers are held accountable.
4. **Privacy:** Safeguard user data and prioritize privacy in all aspects of AI development.
5. **Beneficence:** Design AI systems to promote societal well-being and minimize harm.
6. **Sustainability:** Consider the environmental impact of training and deploying large-scale models.

Governance Strategies

- **Regulatory Compliance:** Align AI development with legal and regulatory standards, such as GDPR or CCPA.
- **Ethics Committees:** Establish internal or external committees to review AI projects for ethical compliance.
- **Stakeholder Engagement:** Involve diverse stakeholders in the design and deployment process to address varied perspectives and concerns.
- **Audits and Certifications:** Conduct regular audits and seek certifications from recognized ethical AI organizations.

Conclusion

The ethical considerations surrounding LLMs are as complex and multifaceted as the models themselves. While these systems hold immense potential to benefit society, their deployment must be guided by principles of fairness, transparency, and accountability. By addressing biases, mitigating misinformation, ensuring privacy, and fostering ethical governance, developers and organizations can build responsible AI systems that empower users and promote societal well-being. As stewards of this transformative technology, we bear the responsibility to navigate these challenges thoughtfully and ethically, ensuring that LLMs serve humanity's best interests.

Part 2: Practical Applications of LLMs

Chapter 5: Prompt Engineering: Unlocking the True Power of LLMs

The Science of Crafting Prompts

The effectiveness of Large Language Models (LLMs) hinges not only on their architectural design and training but also on how they are instructed to perform specific tasks. This is where the science of crafting prompts comes into play. Prompt engineering—the process of designing precise and contextually rich instructions for LLMs—unlocks their true potential. Crafting effective prompts requires an understanding of language patterns, model behavior, and iterative refinement, making it as much an art as it is a science. This chapter explores the principles and methodologies behind prompt engineering, providing insights into how to maximize the utility of LLMs in practical applications.

What Are Prompts and Why Do They Matter?

Prompts are textual inputs provided to an LLM to elicit a specific response. They define the task, set the context, and provide any necessary instructions. For example, a simple prompt might be: "Translate the following sentence into French: The cat is on the table." In response, the LLM would produce: "Le chat est sur la table."

While this example seems straightforward, the power of prompts lies in their versatility and adaptability. By crafting well-designed prompts, users can:

- Direct the model to perform complex tasks.
- Improve response quality and relevance.
- Control the tone, style, or format of the output.
- Handle diverse scenarios with minimal training or fine-tuning.

The efficacy of a prompt can significantly impact the performance of an LLM, making it a crucial aspect of deploying these models effectively.

Core Principles of Crafting Prompts

Creating effective prompts involves adhering to key principles that ensure clarity, relevance, and specificity. These principles serve as the foundation for prompt engineering:

1. Clarity

Ambiguity is the enemy of effective prompts. An unclear or poorly worded prompt can lead to irrelevant or nonsensical outputs. To avoid this:

- Use precise language.

- Clearly define the task and expectations.
- Avoid unnecessary complexity.

Example:

- **Unclear Prompt:** "Summarize this."
- **Clear Prompt:** "Summarize the following text in three sentences, focusing on key events: [Insert text]."

2. Context

Providing context is essential for guiding the model's responses. Contextual information can include background details, examples, or specific constraints.

Example:

- Without context: "Write a poem."
- With context: "Write a four-line poem about the beauty of autumn, using vivid imagery and a reflective tone."

3. Specificity

Specific prompts lead to more focused outputs. Vague instructions can result in generic or off-topic responses.

Example:

- **Vague Prompt:** "Explain gravity."
- **Specific Prompt:** "Explain the concept of gravity in simple terms suitable for a middle school student."

4. Iteration

Prompt engineering often involves iterative refinement. Testing and adjusting prompts based on the model's outputs helps achieve the desired results.

Example: Initial Prompt: "Write a news headline about a recent scientific discovery." Refined Prompt: "Write a concise, engaging news headline about a recent discovery in quantum physics."

Advanced Techniques in Prompt Engineering

Building on these foundational principles, advanced techniques like few-shot learning, chain-of-thought prompting, and Retrieval-Augmented Generation (RAG) enable users to handle complex tasks more effectively.

1. Few-Shot Learning

Few-shot learning involves providing the model with a few examples of the desired output within the prompt. This technique helps the model understand the task and align its responses with user expectations.

Example: Prompt: "Convert the following sentences into passive voice:

1. The cat chased the mouse. → The mouse was chased by the cat.
2. The teacher praised the student. → The student was praised by the teacher.

3. The chef cooked a delicious meal. → "

By including examples, the model is primed to continue the pattern and complete the task accurately.

2. Chain-of-Thought Prompting

Chain-of-thought prompting encourages the model to "think out loud," breaking down its reasoning process step by step. This approach is particularly useful for tasks that require logical reasoning or multi-step calculations.

Example: Prompt: "A store sells apples for $2 each and bananas for $1 each. If a customer buys 3 apples and 5 bananas, how much do they pay in total? Show your reasoning step by step."

Expected Output: "The cost of 3 apples is 3 x $2 = $6. The cost of 5 bananas is 5 x $1 = $5. The total cost is $6 + $5 = $11."

3. Retrieval-Augmented Generation (RAG)

RAG combines LLMs with external knowledge bases or search systems to generate factually accurate and contextually rich outputs. Instead of relying solely on the model's internal knowledge, RAG retrieves relevant information to enhance responses.

Example: Prompt: "Using the latest statistics from the World Health Organization, summarize the global impact of COVID-19."

Here, the model retrieves up-to-date information from a trusted source before generating the response, ensuring accuracy and relevance.

Common Challenges and How to Address Them

While prompt engineering can significantly enhance the performance of LLMs, certain challenges frequently arise. Recognizing and addressing these pitfalls is crucial for success.

1. Ambiguity in Prompts

Ambiguous prompts lead to inconsistent or irrelevant outputs. To address this, ensure that instructions are explicit and leave no room for interpretation.

2. Overly Long Prompts

Lengthy or overly detailed prompts can confuse the model or dilute its focus. Aim for brevity while retaining clarity and context.

3. Ignoring Iteration

Crafting effective prompts often requires multiple iterations. Neglecting this process can result in suboptimal outputs. Embrace a trial-and-error approach, refining prompts based on feedback.

4. Neglecting Model Limitations

LLMs are powerful but not infallible. They may hallucinate information or struggle with highly specialized tasks. Setting realistic expectations and incorporating human oversight can mitigate these limitations.

Applications of Prompt Engineering

Prompt engineering plays a pivotal role in unlocking the full potential of LLMs across various domains:

- **Customer Support:** Crafting prompts for chatbots to handle diverse customer queries effectively.
- **Content Creation:** Generating tailored prompts for producing articles, marketing copy, or creative writing.
- **Education:** Designing prompts to create personalized learning materials or answer student queries.
- **Healthcare:** Developing prompts to assist with summarizing patient records or generating clinical notes.

Future Directions in Prompt Engineering

As LLMs continue to evolve, the field of prompt engineering is expected to advance in several directions:

- **Dynamic Prompting:** Automated systems that adapt prompts based on real-time user inputs or changing contexts.
- **Multimodal Prompting:** Expanding prompts to include visual or auditory elements, enabling richer interactions with multimodal models.
- **Meta-Prompting:** Using prompts to generate other effective prompts, streamlining the process for complex applications.

Conclusion

The science of crafting prompts is a critical skill for leveraging the true power of LLMs. By adhering to core principles, employing advanced techniques, and embracing iterative refinement, users can maximize the utility of these models across diverse applications. As AI technology advances, prompt engineering will remain at the forefront, enabling more intuitive, accurate, and impactful human-AI interactions.

Techniques: Few-Shot Learning, Chain-of-Thought Prompting, and RAG

Effective prompt engineering extends far beyond simply crafting queries. It involves advanced techniques that tap into the latent potential of Large Language Models (LLMs), enabling them to handle diverse, complex, and context-sensitive tasks. Among these techniques, Few-Shot Learning, Chain-of-Thought Prompting, and Retrieval-Augmented Generation (RAG) stand out as transformative tools for maximizing the performance of LLMs. This chapter explores these techniques in detail, examining their principles, applications, and benefits in various contexts.

Few-Shot Learning: Guiding Models Through Examples

Few-Shot Learning enables LLMs to generalize and adapt to specific tasks using only a handful of examples provided within the prompt. This approach is particularly valuable for scenarios where explicit fine-tuning of the model on task-specific data is not feasible.

Principles of Few-Shot Learning

Few-Shot Learning operates on the premise that LLMs can infer patterns and structures from a limited set of examples. When these examples are included in the prompt, they act as a guide, helping the model understand the desired format, tone, and logic of the task at hand.

Example: Prompt: "Translate the following sentences into Spanish:

1. The cat is on the table. → El gato está sobre la mesa.
2. The weather is very nice today. → El clima está muy agradable hoy.
3. I want to buy some fresh bread. →"

Model Output: "Quiero comprar pan fresco."

By providing these examples, the model aligns its output with the demonstrated pattern, producing accurate translations.

Applications of Few-Shot Learning

Few-Shot Learning has broad applications, including:

1. **Text Classification:** Guiding models to classify text into categories using example-labeled inputs.
2. **Style Adaptation:** Demonstrating the tone or style desired for content creation, such as formal writing or casual dialogue.
3. **Data Transformation:** Instructing the model to perform tasks like converting date formats or rephrasing sentences.

Challenges and Considerations

While Few-Shot Learning is highly effective, it is sensitive to the quality and clarity of the examples provided. Poorly chosen examples can confuse the model or lead to inconsistent outputs. Additionally, the token limit of the LLM imposes constraints on the number of examples that can be included in a prompt.

Chain-of-Thought Prompting: Enhancing Logical Reasoning

Chain-of-Thought Prompting is a technique that encourages LLMs to break down complex tasks into smaller, logical steps. By explicitly prompting the model to think through a problem step by step, this method improves accuracy in tasks requiring reasoning, calculation, or decision-making.

Principles of Chain-of-Thought Prompting

This approach leverages the model's ability to maintain and process context over multiple steps. By guiding the model to articulate its reasoning, Chain-of-Thought Prompting reduces errors and increases interpretability.

Example: Prompt: "A store sells apples for $2 each and bananas for $1 each. A customer buys 3 apples and 4 bananas. What is the total cost? Show your reasoning step by step."

Model Output: "The cost of 3 apples is 3 x $2 = $6. The cost of 4 bananas is 4 x $1 = $4. The total cost is $6 + $4 = $10."

By explicitly instructing the model to show its reasoning, Chain-of-Thought Prompting ensures that each step is transparent and logical.

Applications of Chain-of-Thought Prompting

1. **Mathematical Problem Solving:** Breaking down equations or word problems into sequential calculations.
2. **Logical Reasoning Tasks:** Structuring arguments, decision trees, or multi-step analyses.
3. **Debugging Code:** Guiding the model to analyze and identify errors in code snippets by evaluating each line.

Challenges and Limitations

While this method enhances logical reasoning, it can lead to verbose outputs that exceed token limits, particularly in highly complex tasks. Additionally, the quality of the output depends heavily on the clarity of the prompt's instructions.

Retrieval-Augmented Generation (RAG): Combining LLMs with Knowledge Bases

Retrieval-Augmented Generation (RAG) integrates LLMs with external knowledge sources to generate more accurate, contextually rich, and factually grounded outputs. Instead of relying solely on the model's internal parameters, RAG queries external databases or search systems to retrieve relevant information during the generation process.

Principles of RAG

RAG operates in two stages:

1. **Retrieval:** When presented with a query, the system retrieves pertinent information from an external source, such as a document database, knowledge graph, or web search engine.
2. **Generation:** The retrieved information is fed into the LLM as additional context, guiding the model to produce a response that incorporates the external data.

Example: Prompt: "Using the latest statistics from the World Health Organization (WHO), summarize the global impact of COVID-19."

System Workflow:

- The retrieval system queries the WHO database and retrieves recent statistics.
- The LLM generates a summary based on the retrieved data.

Output: "According to the WHO, as of [date], there have been over 500 million confirmed cases of COVID-19 worldwide, with a total of 6.5 million reported deaths. Vaccination efforts have reached 70% of the global population."

Applications of RAG

1. **Research Assistance:** Summarizing and synthesizing information from scientific papers, legal documents, or technical manuals.
2. **Customer Support:** Providing accurate, up-to-date answers by integrating with product documentation or support knowledge bases.

3. **Content Generation:** Enhancing creative or technical writing with facts, references, and citations.

Challenges and Considerations

Implementing RAG systems requires maintaining high-quality, up-to-date external knowledge sources. The retrieval process must be efficient to avoid latency, and the integration between retrieval and generation must ensure coherence and relevance. Additionally, care must be taken to avoid propagating misinformation from unreliable sources.

Comparing the Techniques

While Few-Shot Learning, Chain-of-Thought Prompting, and RAG serve different purposes, they can often complement each other. For example, a RAG system can retrieve domain-specific examples that are then incorporated into Few-Shot Learning prompts. Similarly, Chain-of-Thought Prompting can be enhanced by external data retrieved through RAG, ensuring logical reasoning is supported by factual information.

Technique	Strengths	Challenges
Few-Shot Learning	Quick task adaptation; minimal training required	Sensitive to example quality and token limits
Chain-of-Thought	Improves logical reasoning and interpretability	Verbose outputs; token limit constraints
Retrieval-Augmented Gen	Factually grounded and contextually rich outputs	Dependency on external data quality

Future Directions

As LLM technology evolves, these techniques will continue to be refined and integrated into more sophisticated workflows. Emerging trends include:

- **Dynamic Few-Shot Learning:** Automated systems that dynamically select the most relevant examples based on user queries.
- **Multimodal RAG:** Extending retrieval capabilities to include images, audio, and video alongside text.
- **Hybrid Prompting:** Combining Few-Shot Learning, Chain-of-Thought, and RAG in unified frameworks for complex applications.

Conclusion

Few-Shot Learning, Chain-of-Thought Prompting, and Retrieval-Augmented Generation exemplify the versatility and power of prompt engineering techniques. By leveraging these approaches, users can unlock the full potential of LLMs, enabling them to handle a wide range of tasks with precision, logic, and factual accuracy.

Mastery of these techniques is essential for anyone seeking to harness the transformative capabilities of LLMs in practical, impactful ways.

Common Mistakes and How to Avoid Them

Prompt engineering is a cornerstone of effectively leveraging Large Language Models (LLMs), but it is not without its challenges. Mistakes in crafting prompts can lead to suboptimal performance, irrelevant outputs, or outright failure in achieving desired outcomes. Understanding common pitfalls and how to avoid them is essential for maximizing the utility of LLMs. This chapter identifies the most frequent errors in prompt engineering and provides actionable strategies to mitigate them, ensuring that your interactions with LLMs are both efficient and effective.

Mistake 1: Ambiguous or Vague Prompts

One of the most common mistakes is providing prompts that are unclear or lack specificity. Ambiguous prompts leave too much room for interpretation, leading the model to generate outputs that may not align with the user's intentions.

Example of a Vague Prompt:

"Explain this."

Without additional context, the model cannot discern what "this" refers to, resulting in a generic or irrelevant response.

How to Avoid It:

- **Be Specific:** Clearly define the task, context, and expected output. For example, instead of saying, "Explain this," specify: "Explain the concept of gravity in simple terms for a middle school audience."
- **Provide Context:** Include background information or examples to guide the model. For instance, "Explain the concept of gravity as it relates to objects falling on Earth."

Mistake 2: Overloading the Prompt with Information

While providing context is crucial, overloading the prompt with excessive or irrelevant information can overwhelm the model, diluting the focus and leading to suboptimal outputs.

Example of an Overloaded Prompt:

"Explain gravity, including its history, its mathematical representation, its implications for planetary motion, its role in astrophysics, and its applications in modern technology."

How to Avoid It:

- **Segment the Task:** Break down complex prompts into smaller, manageable parts. For example, ask, "Explain the history of gravity," followed by, "Describe the mathematical representation of gravity."
- **Prioritize Key Information:** Focus on the most critical aspects of the task and provide additional context incrementally if needed.

Mistake 3: Ignoring the Model's Limitations

LLMs are powerful but not omniscient. Assuming that the model can perform tasks beyond its capabilities or generate highly specialized knowledge without proper guidance can lead to unrealistic expectations.

Example of Ignoring Limitations:

"Write a detailed technical report on quantum computing algorithms, including novel research findings."

While the model can provide a general overview, it is unlikely to generate novel research or highly accurate technical details without prior fine-tuning.

How to Avoid It:

- **Set Realistic Expectations:** Understand the model's strengths and weaknesses. Use external tools or resources for tasks requiring highly specialized knowledge.
- **Supplement with External Data:** Incorporate Retrieval-Augmented Generation (RAG) to provide the model with up-to-date and domain-specific information.

Mistake 4: Failing to Test and Iterate

Prompt engineering is an iterative process. A common mistake is assuming that the first prompt will yield the desired result without testing and refining it.

Example of Neglecting Iteration:

Initial Prompt: "Summarize this document."

The output may lack focus or omit critical details if the prompt does not specify the type or depth of the summary required.

How to Avoid It:

- **Iterate on Prompts:** Experiment with variations of the prompt, refining it based on the outputs. For example, revise the initial prompt to: "Summarize this document in three sentences, focusing on key findings and recommendations."
- **Evaluate Outputs:** Analyze the model's responses to identify areas for improvement in the prompt structure.

Mistake 5: Overreliance on Few-Shot Learning

Few-Shot Learning is a powerful technique, but overreliance on it without proper example selection can confuse the model or produce inconsistent outputs.

Example of Poor Few-Shot Learning:

Prompt: "Translate the following sentences into French:

1. I like apples. → J'aime les pommes.
2. The weather is nice. → Le temps est beau.
3. The quick brown fox jumps over the lazy dog."

The third example introduces unnecessary complexity, which can distract the model from the pattern.

How to Avoid It:

- **Choose Relevant Examples:** Ensure that examples are clear, consistent, and directly related to the task.
- **Limit Examples:** Use only as many examples as needed to demonstrate the task without exceeding the model's token limit.

Mistake 6: Ignoring Token Limits

LLMs have a finite token limit for input and output combined. Ignoring this constraint can lead to truncated responses or incomplete outputs.

Example of Ignoring Token Limits:

Prompt: "Generate a detailed analysis of this 10-page document."

If the document exceeds the token limit, the model will not process it fully, leading to an incomplete analysis.

How to Avoid It:

- **Summarize Input:** Condense lengthy inputs into key points or sections before feeding them to the model.
- **Manage Output Length:** Use directives like "summarize" or "provide a concise explanation" to control the output length.

Mistake 7: Neglecting Ethical Considerations

Prompts that inadvertently encourage biased, harmful, or inappropriate outputs can lead to ethical concerns. For example, asking the model to generate stereotypes or misinformation can perpetuate harm.

Example of an Unethical Prompt:

"List reasons why one group is superior to another."

How to Avoid It:

- **Frame Prompts Responsibly:** Ensure that prompts align with ethical guidelines and encourage constructive outputs.
- **Review Outputs:** Monitor and evaluate outputs for unintended bias or harmful content.
- **Incorporate Guardrails:** Use prompt structures that explicitly instruct the model to avoid unethical or biased content.

Mistake 8: Focusing Solely on Syntax Over Semantics

Crafting prompts that are syntactically correct but semantically unclear can confuse the model and lead to irrelevant responses.

Example of a Syntax-Driven Prompt:

"Explain why this is important."

While grammatically correct, the prompt lacks semantic clarity, making it challenging for the model to determine what "this" refers to.

How to Avoid It:

- **Focus on Meaning:** Ensure that prompts convey clear semantic intent. For instance, specify: "Explain why renewable energy is important for combating climate change."

Mistake 9: Overcomplicating Simple Tasks

Adding unnecessary complexity to prompts for straightforward tasks can confuse the model and reduce efficiency.

Example of Overcomplication:

"Provide an exhaustive list of synonyms for 'happy' categorized by context and usage in professional, casual, and poetic scenarios."

How to Avoid It:

- **Simplify Prompts:** Focus on the core objective. For example, "List synonyms for 'happy' suitable for professional and casual contexts."

Mistake 10: Failing to Provide Feedback Mechanisms

Neglecting to incorporate feedback loops into prompt engineering can result in outputs that do not improve over time or adapt to specific needs.

How to Avoid It:

- **Implement Feedback:** Use prompts that solicit user feedback, such as "Does this answer meet your requirements? If not, please specify areas for improvement."
- **Iterative Refinement:** Continuously refine prompts based on user feedback and model performance.

Conclusion

Effective prompt engineering requires an understanding of common mistakes and proactive strategies to address them. By avoiding ambiguity, respecting token limits, leveraging Few-Shot Learning judiciously, and incorporating ethical considerations, users can optimize their interactions with LLMs. Iteration and refinement are integral to the process, ensuring that prompts evolve to meet the dynamic needs of diverse applications. Mastering these principles empowers users to unlock the full potential of LLMs, delivering precise, impactful, and responsible outputs across a wide range of use cases.

Chapter 6: LLMs in Real-World Applications

Building Conversational AI for Business

Conversational AI has emerged as a transformative technology in the business world, enabling organizations to enhance customer experiences, streamline operations, and unlock new opportunities for engagement. Powered by Large Language Models (LLMs), these systems have the ability to understand, interpret, and generate human-like responses, making them invaluable tools for businesses of all sizes. Building conversational AI for business involves a combination of strategic planning, technical implementation, and continuous optimization. This chapter explores the principles, methodologies, and best practices for leveraging LLMs to create effective conversational AI solutions.

The Role of Conversational AI in Business

Conversational AI systems are designed to simulate human conversations, providing automated responses to customer queries, facilitating transactions, and even offering personalized recommendations. Businesses use these systems to:

1. **Enhance Customer Support:** AI-powered chatbots and virtual assistants can handle customer inquiries around the clock, reducing response times and alleviating the workload on human support teams.

2. **Streamline Operations:** Automating repetitive tasks such as appointment scheduling, order tracking, and account management improves efficiency and reduces operational costs.

3. **Drive Sales and Marketing:** Conversational AI can assist with lead generation, product recommendations, and targeted marketing campaigns, providing personalized interactions that boost conversion rates.

4. **Enable Scalability:** Businesses can scale their customer interactions without proportional increases in staffing costs, ensuring consistent service delivery even during peak demand periods.

Key Components of Conversational AI

Building a successful conversational AI system requires integrating several key components:

1. **Natural Language Understanding (NLU):** NLU enables the system to interpret user input, identify intent, and extract relevant information. This involves tokenization, entity recognition, and sentiment analysis.

2. **Dialogue Management:** Dialogue management orchestrates the conversation flow, determining how the system responds to user inputs and maintains context across multiple exchanges.

3. **Natural Language Generation (NLG):** NLG powers the creation of human-like responses, ensuring that the system's outputs are coherent, contextually appropriate, and engaging.

4. **Integration with Backend Systems:** Connecting the AI to databases, CRM platforms, and APIs allows it to fetch and update information, enabling tasks such as order processing and account verification.

5. **User Interface (UI):** The UI—whether a chat window, voice interface, or messaging app—serves as the point of interaction between the user and the conversational AI.

Steps to Building Conversational AI for Business

1. Define Objectives and Use Cases

The first step in building conversational AI is to define its purpose and scope. This involves identifying the specific problems the system will address and the metrics for success.

- **Customer Support Use Case:** Automate responses to FAQs, such as shipping policies or product warranties.
- **Sales Use Case:** Guide customers through product selection and provide personalized recommendations.
- **Operations Use Case:** Automate routine tasks like password resets or appointment scheduling.

2. Choose the Right LLM

Selecting the appropriate LLM is critical to the success of your conversational AI. Factors to consider include:

- **Capabilities:** Assess whether the model supports the desired level of language understanding and generation.
- **Cost and Scalability:** Evaluate the computational resources and costs associated with deploying the model at scale.
- **Customization:** Determine whether the model can be fine-tuned for domain-specific applications.

Popular choices include OpenAI's GPT series for general-purpose applications, Meta's Llama for accessible solutions, and domain-specific models for specialized tasks.

3. Data Preparation and Training

Data is the foundation of any AI system. Preparing high-quality datasets ensures that the conversational AI performs effectively.

- **Gather Data:** Collect historical chat logs, customer queries, and domain-specific documents.
- **Clean and Annotate:** Remove noise, standardize formats, and annotate data for intents, entities, and other relevant features.
- **Fine-Tune the Model:** Customize the LLM on your dataset to align it with your business's unique needs and terminology.

4. Design Conversational Flows

Creating structured conversational flows ensures that the AI can handle various scenarios seamlessly.

- **Intent Mapping:** Define the intents (user goals) the system should recognize, such as "Track Order" or "Reset Password."
- **Context Management:** Design the system to retain context across multiple turns, enabling coherent and meaningful interactions.

- **Fallback Mechanisms:** Implement fallback responses to handle ambiguous or unrecognized inputs gracefully.

5. Develop and Integrate

The development phase involves building the backend and integrating the AI into your existing systems.

- **Backend Development:** Implement APIs to connect the AI with databases and external services.
- **Front-End Integration:** Embed the conversational AI into user-facing platforms like websites, mobile apps, or messaging services.
- **Testing and Debugging:** Conduct extensive testing to identify and resolve issues, ensuring the system operates as intended.

6. Monitor and Optimize

Deploying the AI is not the end of the process. Continuous monitoring and optimization are essential for maintaining performance and relevance.

- **Performance Metrics:** Track key metrics such as response accuracy, resolution rate, and user satisfaction.
- **Feedback Loops:** Incorporate user feedback to identify areas for improvement.
- **Regular Updates:** Update the system to reflect changes in business policies, product offerings, or user preferences.

Best Practices for Building Conversational AI

1. **Start Simple:** Begin with a limited set of use cases and expand functionality incrementally based on user feedback.
2. **Focus on User Experience:** Design the system to be intuitive and user-friendly, ensuring that interactions are seamless and engaging.
3. **Maintain Transparency:** Clearly communicate to users that they are interacting with an AI and provide options for escalation to human agents if needed.
4. **Prioritize Data Privacy:** Adhere to data protection regulations and implement robust security measures to safeguard user information.
5. **Emphasize Accessibility:** Ensure that the conversational AI is accessible to all users, including those with disabilities, by incorporating features like voice input and screen reader compatibility.

Real-World Examples of Conversational AI in Business

1. **E-Commerce:**
    - **Use Case:** Virtual shopping assistants help customers find products, provide recommendations, and answer questions about shipping or returns.
    - **Example:** An online retailer uses an AI chatbot to guide users through the purchasing process, increasing conversion rates.

2. **Banking and Finance:**
   - **Use Case:** Automating routine inquiries such as balance checks, transaction histories, and loan applications.
   - **Example:** A bank deploys a virtual assistant to handle customer inquiries, reducing call center workload and enhancing service availability.

3. **Healthcare:**
   - **Use Case:** Assisting patients with appointment scheduling, symptom checking, and post-treatment follow-ups.
   - **Example:** A hospital uses conversational AI to manage appointment bookings, freeing up administrative staff for other tasks.

4. **Hospitality:**
   - **Use Case:** Answering guest inquiries, processing bookings, and providing local recommendations.
   - **Example:** A hotel integrates a virtual concierge into its app, allowing guests to request services or find nearby attractions easily.

Challenges and How to Overcome Them

1. **Understanding Complex Queries:**
   - **Challenge:** Handling nuanced or multi-faceted queries can be difficult for AI systems.
   - **Solution:** Enhance the system's capabilities through fine-tuning, context management, and fallback mechanisms.

2. **Maintaining Context:**
   - **Challenge:** Losing context in multi-turn conversations can lead to irrelevant or confusing responses.
   - **Solution:** Implement robust context-tracking mechanisms to maintain coherence across interactions.

3. **Ensuring Accuracy:**
   - **Challenge:** Inaccurate or misleading responses can erode user trust.
   - **Solution:** Regularly audit the system's performance and incorporate external validation for critical outputs.

4. **Balancing Automation and Human Oversight:**
   - **Challenge:** Over-automation can lead to frustration in scenarios requiring empathy or complex decision-making.

- **Solution:** Provide clear escalation paths to human agents and define the AI's scope of responsibility.

Future Trends in Conversational AI

As technology evolves, conversational AI is poised to become even more sophisticated and impactful. Key trends include:

- **Multimodal Interactions:** Combining text, voice, and visual inputs to create richer user experiences.
- **Proactive Engagement:** AI systems initiating interactions based on user behavior or preferences.
- **Personalization at Scale:** Leveraging data to deliver highly tailored experiences for individual users.
- **Improved Emotional Intelligence:** Enhancing AI's ability to recognize and respond to user emotions.

Conclusion

Building conversational AI for business is both an art and a science, requiring a strategic approach to design, development, and deployment. By leveraging LLMs effectively, businesses can create systems that enhance customer experiences, streamline operations, and drive growth. With careful planning, continuous optimization, and a commitment to user satisfaction, conversational AI can become a powerful tool for achieving business success in an increasingly digital world.

Creating Search and Recommendation Engines

Search and recommendation engines are indispensable components of the modern digital landscape, powering everything from e-commerce platforms to streaming services and enterprise knowledge systems. Large Language Models (LLMs) have revolutionized how these engines function, offering capabilities far beyond traditional algorithms. By leveraging LLMs, businesses can deliver highly personalized, context-aware, and semantically rich search and recommendation experiences. This chapter explores the principles, applications, and best practices for creating search and recommendation engines powered by LLMs.

The Importance of Search and Recommendation Engines

Search and recommendation systems are designed to help users navigate vast amounts of information and discover relevant content, products, or services. Their role is critical in:

1. **Enhancing User Experience:** Delivering accurate and personalized results improves user satisfaction and engagement.
2. **Driving Business Growth:** Effective recommendations increase conversion rates, sales, and customer retention.
3. **Streamlining Operations:** Efficient search tools enable faster access to information, improving productivity in enterprise settings.

The Role of LLMs in Search and Recommendation Engines

Traditional search and recommendation engines rely heavily on keyword matching, collaborative filtering, and other rule-based algorithms. While effective to an extent, these approaches often struggle with:

- Understanding user intent.
- Capturing semantic nuances.
- Providing personalized experiences.

LLMs address these limitations by:

1. **Understanding Natural Language:** LLMs can interpret and process complex, conversational queries, making search systems more intuitive.
2. **Semantic Matching:** They evaluate the meaning behind words, enabling more accurate matches between queries and content.
3. **Context Awareness:** By retaining and applying context across interactions, LLMs enhance the relevance of recommendations and search results.
4. **Personalization:** LLMs can analyze user behavior and preferences to deliver tailored experiences.

Building Search Engines with LLMs

LLM-powered search engines are designed to go beyond simple keyword matching, offering users an intelligent and dynamic search experience.

1. Query Understanding

Query understanding is the first step in delivering relevant search results. LLMs excel at interpreting user queries, even when they are ambiguous or conversational.

Example: User Query: "What's the best laptop for graphic design under $1,500?"

Traditional systems may focus on keywords like "laptop" and "graphic design," whereas an LLM can:

- Recognize the price constraint.
- Infer that performance specifications (e.g., GPU, RAM) are essential for graphic design.
- Prioritize results that match these criteria.

2. Semantic Search

Semantic search leverages LLMs to match queries with relevant content based on meaning rather than exact word matches. This capability is particularly useful for handling synonyms, paraphrased queries, and nuanced language.

Example: Query: "Best smartphone with a great camera."

Semantic Search Output: Results may include products described as "phones with excellent photography capabilities" or "devices with high-resolution cameras."

3. Contextual Search

Contextual search involves understanding and applying the user's past interactions to refine results. LLMs can maintain context across sessions, enabling more personalized and coherent search experiences.

Example:

- Query 1: "Show me books on space exploration."
- Query 2: "Which ones are suitable for kids?"

An LLM-powered engine understands that the second query refers to children's books about space exploration, refining the results accordingly.

4. Zero-Shot and Few-Shot Learning

LLMs' ability to generalize allows them to handle new or rare queries without extensive retraining. Zero-shot and few-shot learning techniques enable the system to deliver accurate results even for niche topics or emerging trends.

5. Multi-Lingual and Multi-Modal Search

LLMs support multi-lingual queries and multi-modal inputs, allowing users to search across languages and data types (e.g., text, images, and videos).

Example:

- Query: "Find tutorials on creating 3D animations in Spanish."
- Output: Results include Spanish-language video tutorials and written guides.

Developing Recommendation Engines with LLMs

Recommendation engines powered by LLMs provide tailored suggestions by analyzing user behavior, preferences, and contextual factors. These engines can be implemented across domains, including e-commerce, streaming services, and knowledge platforms.

1. Collaborative Filtering with LLMs

Collaborative filtering identifies patterns in user behavior to recommend items that similar users have engaged with. LLMs enhance this process by:

- Identifying latent connections in user preferences.
- Handling sparse or incomplete data more effectively.

Example: An LLM can recommend a niche book to a user based on their reading habits and similarities with other users, even if the book has limited interaction data.

2. Content-Based Recommendations

Content-based recommendation systems suggest items similar to those the user has already interacted with. LLMs' semantic understanding allows them to:

- Analyze product descriptions or metadata.
- Match items based on nuanced features.

Example: A streaming platform using an LLM can recommend movies with similar themes, genres, or narrative styles based on a user's viewing history.

3. Hybrid Recommendation Systems

Combining collaborative filtering and content-based methods, hybrid systems leverage the strengths of both approaches. LLMs act as a unifying layer, integrating diverse data sources and models.

Example: An e-commerce platform might recommend products based on:

- User purchase history (collaborative filtering).
- Product descriptions and reviews (content-based filtering).

4. Real-Time Personalization

LLMs enable dynamic, real-time personalization by analyzing live user interactions. This capability ensures that recommendations evolve with the user's preferences and behaviors.

Example: During an online shopping session, the recommendation engine adapts to the user's browsing patterns, highlighting items that align with their current interests.

Best Practices for Implementing LLM-Powered Systems

To maximize the effectiveness of LLM-powered search and recommendation engines, consider the following best practices:

1. Understand User Needs

- Conduct user research to identify pain points and expectations.
- Design systems that prioritize relevance, speed, and usability.

2. Optimize Data Quality

- Use high-quality, diverse datasets to train and fine-tune LLMs.
- Regularly update data to reflect changing trends and user preferences.

3. Focus on Explainability

- Provide transparent explanations for recommendations or search results.
- Use explainability to build user trust and facilitate feedback.

4. Ensure Scalability

- Optimize infrastructure to handle high query volumes and real-time processing.
- Use scalable architectures like distributed computing for large datasets.

5. Address Bias and Fairness

- Monitor for and mitigate biases in training data and model outputs.
- Implement fairness checks to ensure equitable treatment of diverse user groups.

6. Integrate Feedback Loops

- Continuously gather user feedback to refine algorithms.

- Use reinforcement learning to adapt recommendations based on user interactions.

Challenges and How to Overcome Them

1. Ambiguous Queries

- **Challenge:** Users may provide vague or incomplete inputs.
- **Solution:** Implement clarifying questions or auto-suggestions to guide users.

2. Cold Start Problem

- **Challenge:** Lack of data for new users or items.
- **Solution:** Use LLMs' zero-shot learning capabilities to generate initial recommendations.

3. Scalability Issues

- **Challenge:** High computational demands for processing complex queries.
- **Solution:** Optimize model inference using techniques like quantization or distillation.

Future Trends in LLM-Powered Systems

As LLM technology evolves, search and recommendation engines will continue to advance. Emerging trends include:

- **Voice and Conversational Search:** Integrating voice interfaces and conversational agents for more natural user interactions.
- **Cross-Platform Recommendations:** Providing seamless experiences across devices and platforms.
- **Ethical AI Practices:** Ensuring transparency, accountability, and fairness in recommendations.

Conclusion

Search and recommendation engines powered by LLMs represent a paradigm shift in how users access and interact with information. By leveraging semantic understanding, contextual awareness, and real-time personalization, these systems enhance user experiences and drive business value. With careful implementation and continuous refinement, LLM-powered engines can become indispensable tools for navigating the complexities of the digital world.

Using LLMs with Structured and Unstructured Data

Leveraging Large Language Models (LLMs) with structured and unstructured data has transformed how businesses process, analyze, and derive insights from diverse information sources. While structured data—organized in clear, tabular formats—has traditionally been the backbone of data analytics, unstructured data—such as text, images, and audio—represents the vast majority of digital information. LLMs bridge the gap between these two types of data, enabling seamless integration and unlocking their combined potential for advanced applications.

Understanding Structured and Unstructured Data

Structured Data

Structured data is highly organized and easily searchable within databases. It follows a defined schema, making it ideal for traditional analytics and machine learning tasks.

Examples:

- Customer databases with fields like name, age, and purchase history.
- Financial records in spreadsheets.
- Sensor data from IoT devices.

Characteristics:

- **Defined Schema:** Data adheres to a fixed format (e.g., rows and columns).
- **Ease of Querying:** Structured data can be queried using SQL and similar tools.
- **Applications:** Common in business intelligence, operational analytics, and reporting.

Unstructured Data

Unstructured data lacks a predefined format, making it more challenging to process and analyze. However, it contains rich, context-specific information that can provide valuable insights when effectively utilized.

Examples:

- Emails, social media posts, and chat logs.
- Images, videos, and audio recordings.
- Scientific papers, legal documents, and web pages.

Characteristics:

- **No Fixed Schema:** Data exists in free-form, requiring advanced processing techniques.
- **High Volume:** Represents approximately 80% of all digital data.
- **Applications:** Useful for sentiment analysis, content classification, and predictive modeling.

The Role of LLMs in Bridging Structured and Unstructured Data

LLMs are uniquely positioned to process and integrate structured and unstructured data due to their natural language understanding (NLU) and contextual reasoning capabilities. By transforming unstructured data into analyzable formats and enhancing structured data with contextual insights, LLMs enable a holistic approach to data utilization.

1. Processing Unstructured Data

LLMs excel at extracting meaningful information from unstructured data sources. Techniques such as named entity recognition (NER), summarization, and text classification enable businesses to derive actionable insights from free-form text.

Example:

- **Input:** A corpus of customer reviews.
- **LLM Output:** Extracted insights, such as common complaints, frequently mentioned features, and overall sentiment.

2. Enriching Structured Data

Structured data can be enhanced with insights derived from unstructured data. For example, LLMs can process customer feedback to add sentiment scores or categorize transactions based on contextual information.

Example:

- **Structured Data:** A table of customer transactions.
- **Unstructured Data:** Associated feedback comments.
- **Result:** Enriched dataset with columns for sentiment analysis and categorized topics.

3. Enabling Hybrid Data Models

LLMs facilitate the creation of hybrid data models that combine structured and unstructured data for more comprehensive analysis. These models integrate the precision of structured data with the depth of unstructured insights.

Example:

- In healthcare, patient records (structured data) can be combined with doctor's notes (unstructured data) to improve diagnostics and personalized care recommendations.

Applications of LLMs with Structured and Unstructured Data

1. Customer Experience Optimization

Scenario: A retail company wants to enhance customer satisfaction by analyzing structured sales data alongside unstructured feedback from surveys and social media.

Solution:

- LLMs process survey responses and social media mentions to extract sentiment and recurring themes.
- Structured sales data is enriched with these insights to identify correlations between product performance and customer feedback.
- The result is a prioritized action plan for improving product features and addressing customer concerns.

2. Fraud Detection in Banking

Scenario: A bank aims to identify fraudulent transactions by analyzing structured transaction logs and unstructured support tickets or customer complaints.

Solution:

- LLMs analyze unstructured complaint data to identify patterns or keywords indicative of fraud.

- These findings are integrated into structured transaction data, enabling a hybrid model that flags suspicious activity more effectively.
- By combining these data sources, the system achieves higher accuracy in detecting fraudulent behavior.

3. Knowledge Management in Enterprises

Scenario: A large organization seeks to improve knowledge retrieval by integrating structured metadata from its content management system with unstructured documents and emails.

Solution:

- LLMs process unstructured documents to extract summaries, keywords, and classifications.
- This information is linked with structured metadata, creating a unified knowledge base that supports semantic search.
- Employees can now retrieve relevant information more efficiently, improving productivity and decision-making.

Techniques for Integrating Structured and Unstructured Data with LLMs

1. Feature Engineering

Feature engineering involves extracting relevant features from unstructured data and incorporating them into structured formats for analysis.

Example:

- From customer emails, LLMs extract sentiment scores, urgency levels, and topics. These features are added as new columns in a structured CRM dataset.

2. Embedding Representations

LLMs generate embeddings—dense vector representations—for unstructured data, enabling it to be analyzed alongside structured data in machine learning models.

Example:

- Embeddings generated from product descriptions can be compared with structured sales data to identify trends or anomalies.

3. Data Linking and Annotation

LLMs can link related information across structured and unstructured sources, annotating structured data with insights from unstructured text.

Example:

- In a legal context, LLMs link case metadata (structured) with related case law documents (unstructured), providing comprehensive legal research support.

4. Summarization and Categorization

LLMs summarize unstructured data and categorize it into predefined labels, making it easier to incorporate into structured datasets.

Example:

- LLMs process customer reviews, summarizing each review and tagging it with sentiment and topic labels.

Challenges and Solutions

1. Data Quality Issues

- **Challenge:** Unstructured data often contains noise, inconsistencies, and irrelevant information.
- **Solution:** Implement preprocessing steps such as text cleaning, deduplication, and noise reduction before feeding data into LLMs.

2. Scalability Concerns

- **Challenge:** Processing large volumes of unstructured data with LLMs can be resource-intensive.
- **Solution:** Use optimized models, distributed computing, and batch processing to improve scalability.

3. Integration Complexity

- **Challenge:** Combining structured and unstructured data requires seamless integration and alignment.
- **Solution:** Develop robust pipelines using tools like Apache Spark, TensorFlow, or Hugging Face to streamline integration.

4. Interpretability

- **Challenge:** Outputs generated by LLMs can be challenging to interpret, especially when integrating unstructured insights into structured systems.
- **Solution:** Use explainability techniques to provide context for LLM outputs, ensuring transparency and trust.

Future Trends in LLMs and Data Integration

1. Real-Time Processing

Advances in LLM efficiency will enable real-time analysis and integration of structured and unstructured data, supporting applications such as dynamic pricing and live sentiment analysis.

2. Multimodal Data Integration

Future LLMs will handle multimodal data—text, images, and audio—enabling richer and more holistic data integration.

3. Domain-Specific Models

The development of domain-specific LLMs will enhance the accuracy and relevance of data integration in specialized fields like healthcare, finance, and law.

4. Ethical and Responsible AI

With increasing reliance on LLMs, ensuring ethical use and minimizing biases in data integration will become a top priority.

Conclusion

Using LLMs with structured and unstructured data unlocks unparalleled opportunities for businesses to derive insights and drive innovation. By seamlessly integrating these diverse data types, LLMs enable applications ranging from customer experience optimization to fraud detection and knowledge management. While challenges such as data quality and scalability remain, advancements in LLM technology and best practices will continue to bridge the gap, empowering organizations to harness the full potential of their data assets.

Part 3: Hands-On Development

Chapter 7: Designing and Training Your Own LLM

Step-by-Step Guide to LLM Development

Designing and training your own Large Language Model (LLM) can seem daunting, but breaking it down into structured steps makes the process manageable. LLM development involves careful planning, data preparation, architectural design, training, and evaluation. This guide provides a comprehensive step-by-step approach to developing your own LLM, empowering you to create a model tailored to your specific needs.

Step 1: Define Objectives and Scope

Before embarking on LLM development, clearly outline the purpose and scope of your model. This involves answering key questions such as:

- **What tasks will the LLM perform?** Will it handle text summarization, language translation, question answering, or creative writing?

- **Who is the target audience?** Is the model intended for general use or specialized domains like healthcare, finance, or law?

- **What are the performance benchmarks?** Define success metrics, such as accuracy, latency, or fluency, for evaluating the model.

Setting these objectives ensures that every subsequent step aligns with your end goals.

Step 2: Select or Design the Model Architecture

The choice of architecture significantly influences your model's capabilities. Consider the following options:

1. Transformer-Based Architectures

Modern LLMs are built on transformer architectures due to their efficiency and scalability. Popular options include:

- **GPT (Generative Pre-trained Transformer):** Optimized for text generation and conversational tasks.

- **BERT (Bidirectional Encoder Representations from Transformers):** Focused on understanding tasks like classification and entity recognition.

- **Custom Architectures:** Combine elements from existing architectures to suit your specific requirements.

2. Model Size and Complexity

Decide on the number of layers, attention heads, and parameters. Larger models offer greater capabilities but require more computational resources. For instance:

- Small-scale models (≤100M parameters) are suitable for limited datasets and low-resource environments.
- Large-scale models (≥10B parameters) excel in generalization and fine-tuning for complex tasks.

Step 3: Prepare Datasets for Pretraining and Fine-Tuning

Data is the foundation of any LLM. Preparing high-quality datasets involves several steps:

1. Collect Diverse Datasets

- **Pretraining Data:** Use massive, diverse datasets such as Common Crawl, Wikipedia, and public domain books. Diversity ensures that the model captures a wide range of language patterns and knowledge.
- **Fine-Tuning Data:** Gather domain-specific datasets for tasks like legal document summarization or medical diagnostics.

2. Clean and Preprocess Data

Ensure the data is free from noise, duplicates, and irrelevant content. Common preprocessing tasks include:

- Tokenizing text into subwords or words.
- Removing special characters and irrelevant metadata.
- Converting text to a consistent format, such as lowercasing or standardizing date formats.

3. Annotate Data (If Needed)

For supervised fine-tuning, label the data with relevant tags or classifications. For example, in sentiment analysis, annotate text as positive, negative, or neutral.

Step 4: Implement Data Tokenization and Embedding

1. Tokenization

Tokenization converts raw text into manageable units (tokens) that the model can process. Techniques include:

- **Byte Pair Encoding (BPE):** Efficient for subword tokenization, capturing common prefixes and suffixes.
- **WordPiece or SentencePiece:** Used in models like BERT and T5 for flexible vocabulary generation.

2. Embedding Initialization

Generate initial embeddings for each token to represent them in high-dimensional space. Pretrained embedding libraries like GloVe or FastText can provide a starting point.

Step 5: Configure the Training Environment

Training LLMs requires robust computational infrastructure. Key considerations include:

1. Hardware

- **GPUs/TPUs:** Essential for parallel processing and efficient training. NVIDIA's A100 GPUs or Google's TPUs are popular choices.
- **Distributed Systems:** For large models, use multiple GPUs or nodes to distribute the training workload.

2. Frameworks

Choose machine learning frameworks that support LLM development:

- **PyTorch:** Flexible and widely used for research and development.
- **TensorFlow:** Ideal for production-level deployment.
- **Hugging Face Transformers:** Simplifies model implementation and fine-tuning.

3. Hyperparameter Tuning

Set initial hyperparameters such as:

- Learning rate (e.g., 0.001 for Adam optimizer).
- Batch size (e.g., 64 or 128).
- Number of training epochs (e.g., 10-50 depending on dataset size).

Step 6: Train the Model

1. Pretraining

Pretraining involves training the model on large, unlabeled datasets to learn general language patterns. Techniques include:

- **Masked Language Modeling (MLM):** Masking portions of text and predicting the masked tokens (used in BERT).
- **Causal Language Modeling (CLM):** Predicting the next word in a sequence (used in GPT).

2. Fine-Tuning

Fine-tune the pretrained model on task-specific datasets. This step aligns the model's general knowledge with domain-specific requirements.

3. Monitor Training Metrics

Track metrics like:

- **Loss:** Ensure that training and validation loss decrease steadily.
- **Accuracy/F1-Score:** Evaluate performance on specific tasks.
- **Perplexity:** Measure the model's uncertainty in predicting text.

Step 7: Evaluate the Model

Thorough evaluation ensures that the model meets performance benchmarks. Key evaluation methods include:

1. Quantitative Metrics

- **BLEU/ROUGE Scores:** For text generation and summarization tasks.
- **Precision, Recall, and F1-Score:** For classification tasks.
- **Human Evaluation:** Gather feedback on fluency, coherence, and relevance.

2. Stress Testing

Test the model with edge cases and adversarial inputs to identify weaknesses.

3. Benchmarking

Compare the model against industry-standard benchmarks like GLUE, SQuAD, or SuperGLUE to validate its capabilities.

Step 8: Deploy and Optimize

Once trained and evaluated, the model must be deployed for real-world use:

1. Deployment Strategies

- **APIs:** Serve the model via REST APIs for easy integration.
- **On-Device Deployment:** Optimize smaller models for edge devices.
- **Cloud Deployment:** Use platforms like AWS, Google Cloud, or Azure for scalability.

2. Optimization

Improve efficiency through:

- **Model Pruning:** Remove redundant parameters to reduce size.
- **Quantization:** Convert weights to lower precision (e.g., 16-bit or 8-bit).
- **Distillation:** Train smaller models to mimic larger ones.

Step 9: Monitor and Maintain

1. Continuous Monitoring

Track performance metrics post-deployment to identify and address issues like:

- Model drift.
- Latency or scalability problems.

2. Regular Updates

Fine-tune the model periodically with new data to maintain relevance and accuracy.

Conclusion

Designing and training your own LLM is a complex but rewarding process. By following a structured approach—from defining objectives to deploying and maintaining the model—you can create a system tailored to your specific needs. The key to success lies in meticulous data preparation, careful architectural choices, and iterative evaluation. With the right tools and strategies, you can unlock the full potential of LLMs to drive innovation and deliver impactful solutions.

Preparing Datasets for Pretraining and Fine-Tuning

The quality of a Large Language Model (LLM) hinges on the data it is trained on. Preparing datasets for pretraining and fine-tuning is a critical step in LLM development, as it directly influences the model's performance, generalization ability, and applicability to specific tasks. This process involves sourcing, cleaning, preprocessing, and curating data to ensure it meets the unique requirements of both pretraining and fine-tuning. By understanding the nuances of data preparation, you can create a robust foundation for training effective LLMs.

Understanding the Data Requirements for LLMs

Pretraining Datasets

Pretraining datasets are large-scale and diverse, designed to help the model learn general language patterns, grammar, and contextual relationships. These datasets typically consist of vast amounts of unlabeled text data from various sources.

Characteristics of Pretraining Datasets:

- **Scale:** Billions of tokens are necessary for effective training.
- **Diversity:** Content should cover a wide range of topics, genres, and formats to ensure generalization.
- **Unlabeled Nature:** Pretraining relies on unsupervised learning objectives like Masked Language Modeling (MLM) or Causal Language Modeling (CLM).

Examples of Pretraining Data Sources:

- Wikipedia articles
- Public domain books
- Web scrapes (e.g., Common Crawl)
- News archives and blogs

Fine-Tuning Datasets

Fine-tuning datasets are domain-specific and task-oriented, designed to align the pretrained model with specific applications or objectives.

Characteristics of Fine-Tuning Datasets:

- **Smaller Scale:** Fine-tuning requires fewer examples compared to pretraining.
- **Labeled Data:** Data is annotated for supervised tasks like classification, summarization, or question answering.
- **Domain-Specific:** Data aligns closely with the target domain (e.g., medical texts, legal documents).

Examples of Fine-Tuning Tasks:

- Sentiment analysis using labeled reviews.
- Summarizing scientific papers.
- Translating texts between languages.

Step 1: Sourcing Datasets

1. Open-Source Data Repositories

Leverage publicly available datasets to kickstart your data collection process. Popular repositories include:

- **The Pile:** A large-scale dataset designed for LLM pretraining, comprising academic texts, books, and web data.
- **Common Crawl:** Web scrapes providing diverse content.
- **Hugging Face Datasets:** Pre-curated datasets for various tasks.

2. Domain-Specific Sources

For fine-tuning, gather data from industry-specific sources:

- **Medical Texts:** PubMed and clinical guidelines.
- **Legal Documents:** Case law repositories and government records.
- **Customer Feedback:** Surveys, reviews, and support tickets.

3. Proprietary Data

When available, proprietary data from your organization can provide a competitive edge. Ensure compliance with privacy and ethical guidelines when using sensitive data.

Step 2: Cleaning the Data

Raw data often contains noise, duplicates, and irrelevant content that can hinder training. Data cleaning ensures that the model learns from high-quality inputs.

1. Remove Duplicates

Duplicate entries inflate the dataset size without adding new information, potentially biasing the model. Use tools like Python's pandas library to identify and remove duplicate records.

2. Handle Missing Data

For structured datasets, fill missing values with placeholders or remove incomplete records. For unstructured text, assess whether incomplete data fragments can provide value.

3. Eliminate Irrelevant Content

Filter out non-informative text, such as boilerplate content ("Terms of Service" or "Contact Us" sections), to maintain relevance.

4. Normalize Text

Standardize text to a consistent format by:

- Converting to lowercase.
- Removing special characters and extra spaces.
- Expanding contractions (e.g., "can't" to "cannot").

Step 3: Preprocessing Data

Preprocessing prepares raw data for tokenization and subsequent training. This step involves splitting, organizing, and transforming text into model-ready formats.

1. Tokenization

Tokenization breaks down text into smaller units (tokens), such as words or subwords. Advanced tokenization techniques include:

- **Byte Pair Encoding (BPE):** Efficient for compressing vocabulary while capturing subword patterns.
- **WordPiece or SentencePiece:** Commonly used in transformer models like BERT and T5.

2. Handling Special Characters and Languages

- Remove non-ASCII characters for monolingual models.
- Retain special characters in multi-language datasets to preserve linguistic nuances.

3. Segmenting Long Texts

Split lengthy documents into manageable chunks to fit the model's token limit. For example, divide books into paragraphs or sections.

4. Create Input-Output Pairs (Fine-Tuning)

For supervised fine-tuning tasks, format the data as input-output pairs:

- **Input:** Original text (e.g., "Summarize this article").

- **Output:** Desired response (e.g., "The article discusses...").

Step 4: Annotating Data for Supervised Learning

Annotation involves labeling data to provide ground truth for supervised tasks. This step is essential for tasks requiring structured outputs.

1. Define Annotation Guidelines

- Ensure consistency by creating clear guidelines for annotators.
- Examples: Label reviews as positive, negative, or neutral; tag named entities like organizations and dates.

2. Use Annotation Tools

Leverage tools like Prodigy, Label Studio, or custom-built interfaces to streamline annotation.

3. Quality Control

- Validate annotations through cross-review or majority voting.
- Regularly audit samples to maintain accuracy.

Step 5: Curating Balanced Datasets

Balance is crucial to prevent the model from overfitting to dominant patterns while neglecting minority classes.

1. Avoid Imbalanced Classes

For classification tasks, ensure that all categories are well-represented. Use oversampling, undersampling, or synthetic data generation if necessary.

2. Ensure Topic Diversity

In pretraining, include diverse topics and perspectives to improve generalization.

3. Balance Data Sources

For hybrid datasets combining structured and unstructured data, allocate proportions based on relevance and importance.

Step 6: Evaluate and Validate Data

Before training begins, validate the dataset's quality and suitability:

1. Statistical Analysis

Examine:

- Token distributions.

- Vocabulary size.
- Average sequence lengths.

2. Sample Reviews

Manually review random samples to identify errors or inconsistencies.

3. Small-Scale Testing

Conduct initial tests with a subset of the data to ensure preprocessing and tokenization are functioning correctly.

Step 7: Document the Dataset

Documenting the dataset ensures transparency and reproducibility. Include:

- Data sources and collection methods.
- Preprocessing steps and tools used.
- Annotation guidelines and quality control processes.

Challenges in Data Preparation

1. Data Privacy and Security

Ensure compliance with regulations like GDPR or HIPAA when handling sensitive data. Use anonymization techniques and secure storage.

2. Bias and Fairness

Mitigate biases by curating diverse datasets and auditing for stereotypes or imbalances.

3. Resource Limitations

Large datasets require significant computational resources. Consider leveraging cloud services or optimizing preprocessing pipelines.

Conclusion

Preparing datasets for pretraining and fine-tuning is a meticulous but rewarding process that lays the foundation for effective LLM training. By sourcing high-quality data, cleaning and preprocessing it rigorously, and curating it thoughtfully, you can ensure that your LLM learns accurately and generalizes well across tasks. With careful documentation and continuous validation, your dataset becomes a powerful asset that drives the success of your model.

Hands-On Implementation with Python and PyTorch

Hands-On Implementation with Python and PyTorch

Implementing a large language model (LLM) involves more than just theoretical knowledge; it requires hands-on skills to work with frameworks, tools, and best practices that ensure efficient development and deployment. Python, as a versatile and widely adopted programming language, combined with PyTorch, a flexible deep learning framework, forms a powerful foundation for creating and training LLMs. This guide provides a step-by-step narrative on building and deploying an LLM using Python and PyTorch.

Setting Up the Environment

Before diving into implementation, setting up a robust and reliable development environment is critical. Start by installing the necessary libraries and frameworks:

1. **Install Python:** Ensure you have Python 3.8 or later installed. Use package managers like pyenv or conda for managing Python versions.

2. **Install PyTorch:** Visit the https://pytorch.org/ and follow their instructions for installation based on your system (CPU/GPU) and requirements. For example:

bash

pip install torch torchvision torchaudio --index-url https://download.pytorch.org/whl/cu118

3. **Install Additional Libraries:** For preprocessing, training, and evaluation, install these essential libraries:

bash

pip install numpy pandas transformers datasets

4. **Set Up GPU Acceleration (Optional):** If working with large models, use CUDA for efficient computations. Ensure proper drivers and frameworks (like cuDNN) are installed.

Loading and Preprocessing Data

Data forms the backbone of any LLM project. Using well-structured datasets is essential for effective pretraining and fine-tuning.

1. **Using the datasets Library:** Hugging Face's datasets library provides access to numerous text corpora for training. For example, you can load the Common Crawl dataset:

python

from datasets import load_dataset

```
dataset = load_dataset("cc_news")
```

2. **Tokenization:** Convert raw text into tokenized sequences that the model can process. Use pretrained tokenizers from the transformers library:

python

```
from transformers import AutoTokenizer

tokenizer = AutoTokenizer.from_pretrained("gpt2")

tokenized_data = dataset.map(lambda x: tokenizer(x['text'], truncation=True, padding=True), batched=True)
```

3. **Data Batching:** Prepare data loaders for efficient training. PyTorch's DataLoader handles batching and shuffling:

python

```
from torch.utils.data import DataLoader

def collate_fn(batch):
    return {key: torch.tensor([d[key] for d in batch]) for key in batch[0]}

data_loader = DataLoader(tokenized_data, batch_size=16, collate_fn=collate_fn)
```

Defining the Model Architecture

Defining the architecture is where PyTorch's flexibility shines. For an LLM, a transformer-based architecture (like GPT or BERT) is the standard.

1. **Using Pretrained Models:** Leveraging a pretrained model reduces training time and resource requirements:

python

```
from transformers import AutoModelForCausalLM

model = AutoModelForCausalLM.from_pretrained("gpt2")
```

2. **Customizing the Model:** Modify the architecture if needed. For instance, adding new output layers for a specific task:

python

import torch.nn as nn

model.resize_token_embeddings(len(tokenizer))

3. **Device Management:** Move the model to GPU for accelerated computations:

python

device = torch.device("cuda" if torch.cuda.is_available() else "cpu")

model.to(device)

Training the Model

The training phase involves optimizing the model on the dataset to minimize loss and improve performance.

1. **Define the Optimizer and Scheduler:** PyTorch optimizers like AdamW are well-suited for transformer models:

python

from torch.optim import AdamW

optimizer = AdamW(model.parameters(), lr=5e-5)

Learning rate schedulers can help improve convergence:

python

from transformers import get_scheduler

scheduler = get_scheduler("linear", optimizer=optimizer, num_warmup_steps=100, num_training_steps=len(data_loader) * epochs)

2. **Training Loop:** Implement a training loop that processes batches and updates weights:

python

from torch.nn import CrossEntropyLoss

```python
model.train()
for epoch in range(epochs):
    for batch in data_loader:
        inputs = batch['input_ids'].to(device)
        labels = batch['labels'].to(device)

        outputs = model(inputs, labels=labels)
        loss = outputs.loss
        loss.backward()

        optimizer.step()
        scheduler.step()
        optimizer.zero_grad()
```

3. **Saving Checkpoints:** Periodically save the model to prevent data loss:

python

```python
model.save_pretrained("path_to_save_model")
tokenizer.save_pretrained("path_to_save_tokenizer")
```

Evaluation and Testing

After training, evaluate the model to ensure it meets performance expectations.

1. **Evaluation Dataset:** Use a separate dataset for testing:

python

```python
test_dataset = load_dataset("wikitext", split="test")
```

2. **Metrics:** Common metrics for LLMs include perplexity and accuracy. Compute perplexity as follows:

python

```python
import math
```

```python
model.eval()
with torch.no_grad():
    for batch in test_loader:
        inputs = batch['input_ids'].to(device)
        labels = batch['labels'].to(device)
        outputs = model(inputs, labels=labels)
        loss = outputs.loss
        perplexity = math.exp(loss.item())
print(f"Perplexity: {perplexity}")
```

Fine-Tuning the Model

Fine-tuning allows adapting a general-purpose LLM to specific tasks like summarization or classification.

1. **Loading a Pretrained Model:** Begin with the pretrained weights:

python

```python
model = AutoModelForCausalLM.from_pretrained("gpt2")
```

2. **Task-Specific Datasets:** Load datasets relevant to the fine-tuning task:

python

```python
dataset = load_dataset("cnn_dailymail", "3.0.0")
```

3. **Training Procedure:** Repeat the training process with the new dataset and task-specific objectives.

Deploying the Model

Deployment ensures that the trained model is accessible to users through APIs or other interfaces.

1. **Using Hugging Face Inference API:** Host the model on Hugging Face for quick deployment:

bash

```bash
huggingface-cli login
model.push_to_hub("model_name")
```

2. **Custom API with FastAPI:** Build an API to serve predictions:

```python
from fastapi import FastAPI
from transformers import pipeline

app = FastAPI()
model_pipeline = pipeline("text-generation", model="path_to_model")

@app.post("/predict")
def predict(input_text: str):
    return model_pipeline(input_text)
```

3. **Containerization:** Use Docker to containerize the application for scalability:

```dockerfile
FROM python:3.8
COPY . /app
WORKDIR /app
RUN pip install -r requirements.txt
CMD ["uvicorn", "main:app", "--host", "0.0.0.0", "--port", "8000"]
```

Scaling and Optimizing

1. **Quantization:** Reduce model size and improve latency using tools like ONNX or PyTorch's torch.quantization.
2. **Sharding and Parallelism:** For very large models, use distributed training with PyTorch Distributed Data Parallel (DDP).
3. **Monitoring:** Implement monitoring tools to track usage and performance in real-time.

This hands-on guide with Python and PyTorch provides a comprehensive walkthrough for implementing LLMs, from loading data to deploying the model. The combination of practical coding techniques and industry-standard tools ensures you are well-equipped to create and deploy robust language models for real-world applications.

Chapter 8: Fine-Tuning for Specific Tasks

Supervised Fine-Tuning and Preference Alignment

Fine-tuning large language models (LLMs) is a crucial step in adapting these powerful systems to specific tasks and user requirements. While pretraining equips a model with a broad understanding of language, fine-tuning refines this understanding for targeted applications, ensuring relevance and precision. Supervised fine-tuning and preference alignment are two complementary techniques that maximize the potential of LLMs in real-world scenarios. This chapter explores these processes, their methodologies, and practical applications, offering a comprehensive guide for effectively leveraging fine-tuning in modern AI workflows.

Supervised Fine-Tuning: Building Task-Specific Expertise

Supervised fine-tuning involves training an LLM on labeled datasets to specialize in particular tasks. This process utilizes pairs of inputs and desired outputs, guiding the model to learn specific patterns and relationships within the data.

Key Steps in Supervised Fine-Tuning

1. **Dataset Preparation**

   - Collecting high-quality, task-specific data is the foundation of successful fine-tuning. For example, if you are fine-tuning an LLM for customer support, your dataset might include pairs of user queries and representative responses.

   - Preprocessing is essential to clean and format data. Remove duplicates, handle missing values, and tokenize text appropriately to align with the model's tokenizer.

python

```
from transformers import AutoTokenizer

tokenizer = AutoTokenizer.from_pretrained("gpt2")

tokenized_data = dataset.map(lambda x: tokenizer(x['input'], truncation=True, padding=True), batched=True)
```

2. **Defining the Objective**

   - The fine-tuning objective varies by task. Common objectives include minimizing cross-entropy loss for text generation or optimizing accuracy for classification tasks.

python

```
from torch.nn import CrossEntropyLoss
```

loss_fn = CrossEntropyLoss()

3. **Model Adaptation**
    - Load the pretrained model and add task-specific layers if necessary. For instance, you might add a classification head for sentiment analysis.

python

from transformers import AutoModelForSequenceClassification

model = AutoModelForSequenceClassification.from_pretrained("bert-base-uncased", num_labels=2)

4. **Training Loop**
    - Use the preprocessed dataset to train the model iteratively. Optimizers like AdamW and learning rate schedulers improve convergence.

python

from transformers import AdamW, get_scheduler

optimizer = AdamW(model.parameters(), lr=5e-5)

scheduler = get_scheduler("linear", optimizer=optimizer, num_warmup_steps=100, num_training_steps=len(data_loader) * epochs)

for epoch in range(epochs):
    for batch in data_loader:
        inputs = batch['input_ids'].to(device)
        labels = batch['labels'].to(device)

        outputs = model(inputs, labels=labels)
        loss = outputs.loss
        loss.backward()

        optimizer.step()

```
scheduler.step()

optimizer.zero_grad()
```

Benefits of Supervised Fine-Tuning

- **Task Specialization:** The model becomes proficient in specific tasks, such as summarization, sentiment analysis, or language translation.

- **Improved Performance:** Fine-tuned models often outperform general-purpose models on specific benchmarks.

- **Controlled Behavior:** By defining the output explicitly through labels, fine-tuning ensures predictable and controlled model responses.

Preference Alignment: Aligning Models with Human Expectations

Preference alignment ensures that an LLM not only performs tasks accurately but also aligns its outputs with user preferences and ethical considerations. Unlike supervised fine-tuning, which focuses on specific tasks, preference alignment emphasizes aligning the model's behavior with subjective goals, such as tone, safety, or style.

Why Preference Alignment Matters

- **User Satisfaction:** Outputs that match user preferences lead to a better user experience.

- **Ethical Compliance:** Aligning with societal norms and ethical guidelines prevents harmful or biased outputs.

- **Customization:** Tailoring the model's behavior to specific audiences or use cases enhances its versatility.

Methods for Preference Alignment

1. **Reinforcement Learning with Human Feedback (RLHF)**
    - RLHF combines reinforcement learning with human annotations to guide the model's behavior. Human evaluators score outputs based on quality or alignment, and these scores are used as a reward signal.

python

```
import torch

from transformers import PPOTrainer


trainer = PPOTrainer(
    model=model,
```

```
    tokenizer=tokenizer,
    reward_model=reward_model,
    train_dataset=train_dataset,
)

trainer.train()
```

- For example, in conversational AI, human evaluators may rank model-generated responses based on coherence, politeness, and informativeness.

2. **Preference Modeling**
   - Develop a preference model that predicts the likelihood of human approval for a given output. This model is trained on a dataset of labeled preferences and used to guide the LLM during generation.

```python
from transformers import AutoModelForSequenceClassification

preference_model = AutoModelForSequenceClassification.from_pretrained("bert-base-uncased")
preference_model.train()
```

3. **Iterative Feedback Loops**
   - Allow end-users to provide feedback on the model's outputs post-deployment. Continuously integrate this feedback to refine the model.

```python
feedback = collect_user_feedback()  # Hypothetical function
update_model(preference_model, feedback)
```

Challenges in Preference Alignment

- **Subjectivity:** Human preferences are often subjective, making consistent annotations difficult.
- **Scalability:** Scaling human feedback for large datasets can be resource-intensive.
- **Bias:** Human annotations may inadvertently introduce biases, which require mitigation strategies.

Practical Applications

1. **Customer Support**
   - Fine-tuned and preference-aligned LLMs provide empathetic, accurate, and contextually relevant responses to customer queries.
   - Preference alignment ensures the tone remains professional and friendly.

2. **Content Moderation**
   - Models can be fine-tuned to identify and filter inappropriate content. Preference alignment ensures outputs comply with platform policies.

3. **Healthcare Applications**
   - In medical chatbot applications, fine-tuning ensures accuracy in diagnoses, while preference alignment tailors advice to cultural or individual sensitivities.

Combining Supervised Fine-Tuning and Preference Alignment

While supervised fine-tuning provides the foundational task-specific skills, preference alignment refines the model to better meet user expectations. Combining these techniques yields powerful LLMs capable of excelling in diverse applications.

Case Study: Developing a Personalized AI Writing Assistant

1. **Dataset Preparation:**
   - Collect examples of well-written essays, emails, and reports.
   - Annotate examples with labels indicating tone, clarity, and professionalism.

2. **Fine-Tuning:**
   - Train the model on the labeled dataset to generate coherent and structured text for specific genres.

3. **Preference Alignment:**
   - Gather feedback from beta users on the generated outputs, ranking them based on satisfaction.
   - Use RLHF to refine the model's behavior, ensuring it adheres to user preferences.

4. **Deployment:**
   - Deploy the model as a cloud-based API, allowing users to input preferences like tone (formal/informal) and style (creative/technical).

Best Practices for Fine-Tuning and Alignment

1. **Iterate Gradually:**
    - Start with small datasets and gradually scale up as performance improves.
2. **Monitor Biases:**
    - Regularly evaluate the model for unintended biases introduced during training or alignment.
3. **Leverage Transfer Learning:**
    - Utilize pretrained models as a base to save resources and accelerate development.
4. **Engage Users:**
    - Involve end-users in the alignment process to ensure outputs meet their expectations.

Supervised fine-tuning and preference alignment are transformative tools in adapting LLMs to meet specific requirements. By mastering these techniques, developers can create models that excel in accuracy, relevance, and user satisfaction, ensuring their outputs are not only functional but also tailored to the needs and expectations of their target audience.

Leveraging Transfer Learning for Efficiency

The concept of transfer learning has revolutionized the field of machine learning, especially in the development of large language models (LLMs). By leveraging the knowledge learned from one domain or task and applying it to another, transfer learning significantly reduces the time, computational resources, and data requirements for building high-performing models. This efficiency makes transfer learning an indispensable tool in training and fine-tuning LLMs for specific applications.

In this chapter, we will explore the fundamentals of transfer learning, its benefits, its integration into LLM workflows, and practical techniques for maximizing efficiency in real-world applications.

Understanding Transfer Learning

Transfer learning involves taking a model pretrained on a vast dataset and adapting it to a narrower, domain-specific task. For LLMs, this means utilizing a model like GPT-3, BERT, or Llama, which has already been trained on diverse and extensive datasets such as Common Crawl, Wikipedia, or BooksCorpus. This pretrained model serves as a foundation, allowing developers to fine-tune it for specialized applications.

Key Components of Transfer Learning

1. **Pretraining:**
    - Pretraining is the first phase, where a model learns general linguistic patterns, contextual relationships, and syntactic rules from large-scale datasets. This stage requires significant computational resources and time.
2. **Fine-Tuning:**

- Fine-tuning involves adapting the pretrained model to a specific domain or task, such as sentiment analysis, customer support chatbots, or medical report generation. This stage is far less resource-intensive because the model already possesses foundational knowledge.

3. **Feature Transfer:**
    - In the context of LLMs, feature transfer leverages embeddings, attention mechanisms, and learned parameters from the pretrained model, which can be directly applied to new tasks.

Why Transfer Learning is Efficient

1. Reduction in Data Requirements

- Training an LLM from scratch requires immense amounts of data. For example, GPT-3 was trained on hundreds of gigabytes of text. However, transfer learning enables fine-tuning with as little as a few thousand labeled examples, making it accessible for niche tasks with limited data availability.

2. Time and Cost Efficiency

- The pretraining phase of LLMs is computationally expensive, often requiring weeks on high-performance GPUs or TPUs. By starting with a pretrained model, developers bypass this step and focus resources on fine-tuning, reducing both time and cost.

3. Improved Performance on Specialized Tasks

- Pretrained LLMs already understand linguistic nuances and general world knowledge, allowing them to excel at specific tasks after fine-tuning. This is particularly valuable for domains like legal, medical, or technical writing, where precision and expertise are critical.

4. Scalability Across Domains

- Transfer learning allows a single pretrained model to be fine-tuned for multiple tasks or domains. For instance, a model like GPT-3 can be adapted for chatbots, summarization, or code generation with minimal additional effort.

Practical Techniques for Leveraging Transfer Learning

1. Choosing the Right Pretrained Model

Selecting the appropriate base model is crucial for effective transfer learning. Consider factors such as the model's size, architecture, and training data.

- **For General Applications:** Models like GPT-3 and BERT are versatile and can be fine-tuned for a wide range of tasks.
- **For Domain-Specific Applications:** Use models pretrained on domain-relevant datasets. For example, SciBERT is ideal for scientific text, while ClinicalBERT excels in healthcare contexts.

2. Feature Extraction

In some cases, you can freeze the pretrained layers of a model and use them as feature extractors, only training the task-specific output layers. This approach minimizes computational requirements.

python

```
from transformers import AutoModel, AutoTokenizer

# Load pretrained model
model = AutoModel.from_pretrained("bert-base-uncased")
tokenizer = AutoTokenizer.from_pretrained("bert-base-uncased")

# Freeze all layers
for param in model.parameters():
    param.requires_grad = False

# Add custom classification head
import torch.nn as nn
model.classifier = nn.Linear(model.config.hidden_size, num_labels)
```

3. Fine-Tuning with Smaller Learning Rates

Fine-tuning pretrained models requires careful adjustment of the learning rate. Typically, smaller learning rates (e.g., 1e-5 to 5e-5) are used to avoid catastrophic forgetting—where the model loses its general knowledge.

python

```
from transformers import AdamW

optimizer = AdamW(model.parameters(), lr=2e-5)
```

4. Data Augmentation

When data is scarce, augmentation techniques like paraphrasing, back-translation, or synonym replacement can expand the dataset and improve fine-tuning results.

5. Parameter-Efficient Fine-Tuning

Recent techniques like LoRA (Low-Rank Adaptation) and adapters enable efficient fine-tuning by modifying only a subset of model parameters. These methods drastically reduce memory usage while maintaining performance.

Case Study: Transfer Learning for Sentiment Analysis

Problem Statement

A retail company wants to build a sentiment analysis tool to classify customer reviews as positive, neutral, or negative.

Step 1: Select a Pretrained Model

- BERT is chosen as the base model due to its strong performance on text classification tasks.

Step 2: Prepare the Dataset

- The company collects 5,000 labeled customer reviews and preprocesses them for tokenization.

Step 3: Fine-Tune the Model

- The pretrained BERT model is loaded, and a classification head is added. The model is fine-tuned for five epochs with a learning rate of 3e-5.

python

```
from transformers import BertForSequenceClassification

model = BertForSequenceClassification.from_pretrained("bert-base-uncased", num_labels=3)
```

Step 4: Evaluate and Deploy

- After achieving 95% accuracy on a validation set, the model is deployed via an API for integration with the company's analytics platform.

Advanced Techniques for Optimizing Transfer Learning

1. Multi-Task Learning

Train a model on multiple related tasks simultaneously to improve generalization. For example, train a model for sentiment analysis and intent detection together.

2. Active Learning

Use active learning to prioritize labeling the most informative examples, reducing the amount of labeled data needed for fine-tuning.

3. Continual Learning

Continually fine-tune the model as new data becomes available, ensuring it stays relevant and accurate over time.

4. Distributed Training

Leverage distributed training frameworks like PyTorch Lightning or Hugging Face Accelerate to speed up fine-tuning across multiple GPUs.

Challenges in Transfer Learning

1. Domain Shift

A significant difference between the pretraining dataset and the fine-tuning dataset can lead to suboptimal performance. Address this by selecting a model pretrained on domain-relevant data or augmenting the fine-tuning dataset.

2. Overfitting

Small datasets in fine-tuning can cause overfitting. Techniques like dropout regularization and early stopping help mitigate this issue.

3. Computational Requirements

Although transfer learning is more efficient than training from scratch, it still requires substantial computational resources for fine-tuning large models.

Conclusion

Transfer learning has become a cornerstone of modern machine learning, enabling efficient and effective adaptation of LLMs for diverse applications. By building on the foundational knowledge of pretrained models, developers can unlock the full potential of LLMs while saving time, resources, and effort. From small-scale sentiment analysis tools to large-scale domain-specific applications, transfer learning bridges the gap between general-purpose models and specialized real-world tasks, ensuring relevance, accuracy, and scalability.

Case Study: Customizing an LLM for Your Needs

Customizing a large language model (LLM) to meet specific requirements is a transformative step in applying artificial intelligence to real-world challenges. The adaptability of LLMs makes them invaluable across industries, from healthcare to e-commerce, but success often hinges on effectively tailoring a model to a unique problem. In this case study, we'll explore the end-to-end process of customizing an LLM, walking through a practical example: developing a personalized AI assistant for a legal firm. The narrative illustrates best practices, challenges, and solutions for creating a highly specialized, effective, and efficient model.

Understanding the Problem

Client Requirements

A mid-sized legal firm wants an AI assistant to streamline document analysis and case preparation. The model needs to:

- Extract key points from legal documents.
- Summarize case law in plain English.
- Answer queries related to specific statutes and precedents.
- Maintain a formal tone, ensuring accuracy and professionalism.

Challenges

1. **Domain-Specific Knowledge:** General-purpose LLMs lack in-depth expertise in legal terminology and case law.
2. **High Accuracy Needs:** The legal field requires precision, as mistakes can have significant consequences.
3. **Scalability:** The model must handle large document datasets efficiently.

Step 1: Selecting the Base Model

The first step in customization is choosing an appropriate pretrained LLM. After evaluating options, the legal firm selects **BERT-Legal**, a variant of BERT pretrained on legal texts, for its robust understanding of legal jargon and structure.

Why BERT-Legal?

- Trained on domain-specific data, such as court cases, legal statutes, and contracts.
- Optimized for tasks like question answering, classification, and summarization.
- Pretrained on datasets like EUR-Lex and Harvard Case Law Corpus, ensuring a strong foundation.

Step 2: Preparing the Dataset

Dataset Collection

The legal firm provides:

1. A corpus of anonymized legal documents, including contracts, pleadings, and case summaries.
2. FAQs based on commonly asked legal queries.
3. Annotated examples of ideal summaries and responses.

Preprocessing

The raw data undergoes cleaning and formatting:

1. **Text Cleaning:** Remove metadata, formatting artifacts, and non-relevant sections like footnotes.
2. **Tokenization:** Use the pretrained tokenizer compatible with BERT-Legal:

python

```
from transformers import AutoTokenizer

tokenizer = AutoTokenizer.from_pretrained("nlpaueb/legal-bert-base-uncased")
tokenized_data = dataset.map(lambda x: tokenizer(x['text'], truncation=True, padding=True), batched=True)
```
   3. **Labeling:** Annotate data with labels for tasks like summarization (input_text -> summary) and question answering (query -> answer).

Augmentation

To expand the dataset:

- Synonym replacement ensures variability in phrasing.
- Paraphrasing tools rewrite text while retaining meaning.

Step 3: Fine-Tuning the Model

Fine-tuning adapts the pretrained model to the firm's specific tasks.

Task-Specific Fine-Tuning

   1. **Text Summarization**
      - Objective: Summarize lengthy case documents into concise briefs.
      - Implementation:
        - Use labeled summaries as the target output.
        - Fine-tune with a supervised learning approach:

python
```
from transformers import BartForConditionalGeneration

model = BartForConditionalGeneration.from_pretrained("facebook/bart-large")
model.train()
```
      - Evaluation: Measure performance using ROUGE scores to ensure summaries capture critical information.

   2. **Question Answering**
      - Objective: Enable the model to retrieve accurate answers from legal texts.
      - Implementation:

- Train using a question-answer dataset, where inputs are queries and outputs are spans of text from source documents.

python

from transformers import AutoModelForQuestionAnswering

model = AutoModelForQuestionAnswering.from_pretrained("nlpaueb/legal-bert-base-uncased")

- Evaluation: Use metrics like F1 score and exact match (EM) to assess performance.

3. **Document Classification**
   - Objective: Categorize legal documents (e.g., contracts, pleadings, briefs).
   - Implementation:
     - Add a classification head and fine-tune for multi-class text classification.

python

from transformers import AutoModelForSequenceClassification

model = AutoModelForSequenceClassification.from_pretrained("nlpaueb/legal-bert-base-uncased", num_labels=5)

Step 4: Evaluating the Model

Evaluation ensures that the fine-tuned model meets the firm's standards.

Metrics

1. **Summarization Tasks:**
   - ROUGE-1, ROUGE-2, and ROUGE-L scores evaluate how well the generated summaries match reference texts.

2. **Question Answering Tasks:**
   - F1 Score: Measures the overlap between predicted and true answers.
   - Exact Match: Verifies whether predictions exactly match ground truth.

3. **Classification Tasks:**
   - Accuracy: Assesses the percentage of correct predictions.
   - Precision, Recall, and F1 Score: Provide deeper insights into classification performance.

Human Evaluation

The firm's legal team reviews model outputs for accuracy, relevance, and tone. Feedback loops refine performance.

Step 5: Deployment

After successful evaluation, the model is prepared for deployment.

API Development

An API interface allows the firm to integrate the AI assistant into its existing workflow. Using **FastAPI**, the model is deployed as a RESTful service:

```python
from fastapi import FastAPI
from transformers import pipeline

app = FastAPI()
qa_pipeline = pipeline("question-answering", model=model, tokenizer=tokenizer)

@app.post("/answer")
def answer_question(question: str, context: str):
    return qa_pipeline(question=question, context=context)
```

Scaling and Optimization

To handle large datasets:

1. **Distributed Processing:** Leverage libraries like Ray or Dask.
2. **Batch Processing:** Process multiple documents concurrently to improve throughput.
3. **Quantization:** Reduce the model's size without significant performance loss using PyTorch's quantization utilities.

Step 6: Post-Deployment Monitoring and Updates

Deploying the model is not the end of the journey. Continuous monitoring ensures the AI assistant remains effective and relevant.

Monitoring

1. **Performance Tracking:** Track key metrics like response time, accuracy, and user satisfaction.
2. **Error Analysis:** Identify and address failure cases through periodic audits.

Feedback Loop

The legal team provides feedback on problematic outputs, which are added to the training dataset for incremental fine-tuning.

Regular Updates

As legal texts evolve, the dataset and model are updated to reflect new statutes and case law.

Outcomes

The customized AI assistant delivers tangible benefits:

1. **Efficiency Gains:** Reduces the time spent on document analysis by 70%.
2. **Enhanced Accuracy:** Provides reliable summaries and answers with minimal errors.
3. **Scalability:** Handles a growing workload without compromising performance.

Best Practices for Customizing LLMs

1. **Understand the Problem Domain:**
   - Collaborate with domain experts to ensure the dataset and outputs align with real-world requirements.
2. **Leverage Pretrained Models:**
   - Use domain-specific pretrained models to save time and improve task-specific performance.
3. **Iterate with Feedback:**
   - Incorporate user feedback to refine model outputs and improve user satisfaction.
4. **Monitor Continuously:**
   - Regularly evaluate and update the model to maintain relevance and accuracy.

This case study demonstrates the power of customizing LLMs for specific needs. By following a structured approach—selecting the right model, preparing high-quality data, fine-tuning effectively, and deploying thoughtfully—developers can create AI systems that deliver exceptional value in demanding fields like law, medicine, or finance.

Part 4: Deploying LLMs for Production

Chapter 9: From Prototype to Production

Creating Scalable and Modular LLM Solutions

Creating Scalable and Modular LLM Solutions

Deploying large language models (LLMs) in production environments involves challenges far beyond initial development. While building prototypes is an iterative and creative process, production systems require scalability, modularity, and robustness to handle real-world demands effectively. In this chapter, we explore best practices and strategies for creating scalable and modular LLM solutions, focusing on design principles, infrastructure, and workflows that ensure seamless deployment, maintenance, and scaling.

The Need for Scalability and Modularity

Scalability: Meeting Growing Demands

As applications powered by LLMs grow in popularity, their workloads can increase exponentially. Whether serving thousands of simultaneous chatbot queries or processing terabytes of data for document summarization, LLM solutions must scale without degrading performance or breaking down.

Modularity: Flexibility and Maintainability

A modular design enables developers to build solutions that are easier to understand, debug, and update. By isolating key components—such as data preprocessing, model inference, and API serving—developers can enhance flexibility and reduce the complexity of updates or feature additions.

Design Principles for Scalable and Modular LLM Solutions

1. Component-Based Architecture

Divide the system into distinct components that handle specific tasks. Typical components include:

1. **Preprocessing Module:** Cleans and tokenizes input data.
2. **Inference Engine:** Runs the LLM and generates predictions.
3. **Postprocessing Unit:** Formats and structures outputs for end-user consumption.
4. **API Gateway:** Interfaces with clients for input and output exchange.

By decoupling these components, each can be developed, scaled, and updated independently.

2. Stateless Services

Design services to be stateless, meaning they do not retain information between requests. Statelessness ensures scalability by allowing multiple instances of a service to run concurrently without the need for synchronization.

3. Microservices Architecture

Use a microservices approach where each module operates as an independent service. For instance, a model serving endpoint could run separately from a feature extraction pipeline. Tools like Docker and Kubernetes make deploying and managing these microservices efficient.

4. Asynchronous Workflows

For high-throughput systems, asynchronous processing is essential. Queue-based architectures, using tools like RabbitMQ or AWS SQS, can decouple tasks and ensure that each module operates independently without bottlenecks.

Infrastructure for Scalable LLM Solutions

1. Cloud-Native Platforms

Cloud platforms like AWS, Google Cloud, and Azure are critical for scalability. They provide the flexibility to deploy solutions globally and scale dynamically based on demand.

1. **Elastic Compute Services:** Use services like AWS EC2 or Google Cloud Compute Engine for scalable compute resources.
2. **Serverless Options:** AWS Lambda or Google Cloud Functions allow running small tasks without managing servers, ideal for preprocessing or postprocessing.

2. Kubernetes for Orchestration

Kubernetes is the industry standard for container orchestration, enabling scalable deployments of LLM applications. It handles load balancing, scaling, and failover automatically.

- **Example:** Deploying an inference service as a Kubernetes pod:

yaml

apiVersion: apps/v1

kind: Deployment

metadata:

 name: llm-inference-service

spec:

 replicas: 3

 template:

  spec:

```
containers:
- name: llm-inference
  image: llm-inference:latest
  resources:
    limits:
      memory: "4Gi"
      cpu: "2000m"
```

3. Distributed Systems for Parallel Processing

To handle massive datasets or requests, distributed systems such as Apache Spark can process data across multiple nodes in parallel. For instance, batch tokenization of a billion documents can be distributed for faster throughput.

4. Load Balancers and Auto-Scaling

Incorporate load balancers like AWS Elastic Load Balancing (ELB) to distribute incoming traffic across multiple servers. Combine this with auto-scaling groups to dynamically adjust the number of active instances based on traffic.

Strategies for Efficient Inference

Inference, the process of generating predictions from an LLM, is computationally expensive. Efficient inference strategies can significantly enhance scalability.

1. Model Optimization

1. **Quantization:** Reduce model precision (e.g., float32 to int8) to decrease memory usage and accelerate computations.
2. **Pruning:** Remove redundant parameters from the model without compromising accuracy.

2. Batch Inference

Batch multiple requests together for processing, leveraging the parallelism of GPUs or TPUs. Frameworks like PyTorch and TensorRT support batch inference natively.

3. Model Sharding

Split large models across multiple GPUs or machines. Each shard processes a portion of the model, enabling inference for models too large to fit on a single device.

4. Cached Responses

For frequently repeated queries, use caching mechanisms to return precomputed responses instead of running inference again.

Ensuring Modularity with APIs and Tools

1. REST and GraphQL APIs

Develop APIs to allow seamless integration with external applications. A REST API can handle standard CRUD operations, while GraphQL offers more flexibility for complex data querying.

2. Orchestrating Pipelines with Workflow Tools

Workflow orchestration tools like Apache Airflow or Prefect allow defining and managing complex, modular pipelines. For example, a pipeline might consist of:

1. Data ingestion and preprocessing.
2. LLM inference.
3. Result aggregation and storage.

```python
from airflow import DAG
from airflow.operators.python import PythonOperator


def preprocess_data():
    # Preprocessing logic here
    pass


def run_inference():
    # LLM inference logic here
    pass


with DAG("llm_pipeline", schedule_interval=None) as dag:
    preprocess = PythonOperator(task_id="preprocess", python_callable=preprocess_data)
    inference = PythonOperator(task_id="inference", python_callable=run_inference)

    preprocess >> inference
```

Scaling Strategies for LLM Applications

1. Horizontal Scaling

Add more instances of a service to handle increased workloads. Horizontal scaling is particularly effective for stateless services like inference endpoints.

2. Vertical Scaling

Upgrade the compute power of individual instances by increasing CPU, GPU, or memory resources. This approach works well for tasks like training or large-scale batch inference.

3. Geographical Scaling

Deploy services across multiple regions to reduce latency for users around the world. Use CDNs (Content Delivery Networks) for fast delivery of static assets.

4. Multi-Tenancy

Design systems to handle multiple tenants (e.g., customers or applications) by isolating data and processing for each tenant while sharing underlying resources.

Monitoring and Debugging Scalable Systems

Scalable systems require robust monitoring to ensure they operate efficiently under varying workloads.

1. Observability Tools

- **Metrics Collection:** Use tools like Prometheus or AWS CloudWatch to track CPU, memory, and GPU usage.
- **Log Management:** Centralize logs with Elasticsearch or Splunk for real-time analysis.
- **Tracing:** Tools like Jaeger or OpenTelemetry provide insights into the flow of requests through the system.

2. Alerting Systems

Set up automated alerts for critical thresholds, such as high latency or low availability.

3. Debugging Distributed Systems

Debugging becomes complex in distributed systems. Use logging and tracing tools to pinpoint failures and bottlenecks.

Example: Scalable LLM Deployment for Customer Support

Scenario

An e-commerce company deploys an LLM-powered chatbot for customer support, expected to handle 10,000 concurrent queries during peak hours.

Implementation

1. **Modular Design:** Separate services for query preprocessing, model inference, and response postprocessing.
2. **Kubernetes Deployment:** Deploy each service as a containerized microservice managed by Kubernetes.
3. **Autoscaling:** Configure auto-scaling rules to add pods dynamically during traffic spikes.
4. **Caching:** Cache frequent queries, such as "What is your return policy?"
5. **Monitoring:** Use Prometheus and Grafana dashboards to visualize system health.

Outcome

The modular and scalable design ensures low latency (under 200 ms per query) and high availability, even during Black Friday sales.

Conclusion

Creating scalable and modular LLM solutions is an essential skill for deploying AI systems that meet real-world demands. By adopting component-based architectures, leveraging cloud-native infrastructure, and optimizing inference workflows, developers can build robust systems capable of handling dynamic workloads. With the strategies outlined in this chapter, you are equipped to design LLM solutions that are not only powerful but also reliable, efficient, and ready for production.

Infrastructure as Code (IaC) with AWS and Other Tools

Deploying large language models (LLMs) in production requires robust, scalable, and efficient infrastructure. The complexity of managing cloud resources, networks, and deployment environments can be significantly reduced by adopting **Infrastructure as Code (IaC)**. IaC is a paradigm that enables the provisioning and management of infrastructure using declarative code, ensuring consistency, scalability, and repeatability.

In this chapter, we will delve into the principles of IaC, its application using AWS and other tools, and the best practices to build production-ready infrastructure for LLM deployments.

Why Infrastructure as Code is Essential for LLM Deployments

1. Scalability

LLM applications often require dynamic scaling to handle fluctuating workloads. IaC automates the provisioning of resources like virtual machines, storage, and networking to scale up or down as needed.

2. Consistency

Manually configuring infrastructure is error-prone and inconsistent. IaC ensures that environments remain identical across development, testing, and production by codifying configurations.

3. Repeatability

IaC enables developers to replicate infrastructure effortlessly, whether for disaster recovery, staging environments, or multi-region deployments.

4. Cost Optimization

By automating resource provisioning and decommissioning, IaC minimizes idle resources and optimizes costs.

Key Concepts of IaC

1. **Declarative vs. Imperative Approaches**
   - **Declarative IaC:** Defines the desired state of infrastructure (e.g., "I need an EC2 instance"). Tools like AWS CloudFormation and Terraform follow this approach.
   - **Imperative IaC:** Describes the steps to achieve a desired state (e.g., "Start an EC2 instance, then configure it"). Tools like Ansible often use this style.

2. **State Management**
   - IaC tools maintain a "state file" to track the current state of infrastructure. This state ensures changes are applied incrementally and prevents conflicts.

3. **Version Control**
   - IaC files can be stored in Git repositories, enabling collaboration, versioning, and rollback capabilities.

Getting Started with IaC on AWS

1. AWS CloudFormation

AWS CloudFormation is a native IaC tool that allows you to define and provision AWS resources using templates written in JSON or YAML.

Example: Deploying an EC2 Instance

yaml

Resources:

  MyEC2Instance:

    Type: AWS::EC2::Instance

    Properties:

      InstanceType: t2.micro

      ImageId: ami-0abcdef1234567890

Steps:

1. Write the CloudFormation template.
2. Upload the template to the AWS Management Console.
3. Create a stack to deploy resources as defined in the template.

2. Terraform

Terraform is a popular IaC tool that supports multiple cloud providers, including AWS, Google Cloud, and Azure. It uses a declarative configuration language (HCL).

Example: Deploying an EC2 Instance with Terraform

hcl

```
provider "aws" {
  region = "us-west-2"
}


resource "aws_instance" "example" {
  ami           = "ami-0abcdef1234567890"
  instance_type = "t2.micro"
}
```

Steps:

1. Install Terraform and configure AWS credentials.
2. Write the configuration file (e.g., main.tf).
3. Initialize Terraform:

bash

Copia codice

```
terraform init
```

4. Apply the configuration:

bash

```
terraform apply
```

3. AWS CDK (Cloud Development Kit)

AWS CDK enables you to define infrastructure using familiar programming languages like Python, TypeScript, and Java.

Example: Deploying an S3 Bucket with AWS CDK (Python)

```python
from aws_cdk import core
from aws_cdk.aws_s3 import Bucket

class MyStack(core.Stack):
    def __init__(self, scope: core.Construct, id: str, **kwargs):
        super().__init__(scope, id, **kwargs)
        Bucket(self, "MyBucket")

app = core.App()
MyStack(app, "MyStack")
app.synth()
```

Benefits:

- Familiar syntax for developers.
- Reusability and modularity through constructs.

Key Features for LLM Deployments with AWS

1. Compute Resources

- **EC2 Instances:** Ideal for running inference with GPU acceleration.
- **AWS Lambda:** For serverless preprocessing or postprocessing tasks.
- **Amazon SageMaker:** Specialized for training and deploying machine learning models.

2. Storage Solutions

- **Amazon S3:** For storing datasets, model weights, and logs.
- **Amazon EFS:** Provides scalable, shared file storage for distributed LLM training.

3. Networking

- **VPC (Virtual Private Cloud):** Ensures secure, isolated environments for your infrastructure.
- **Elastic Load Balancer:** Distributes incoming traffic across multiple instances for high availability.

4. Monitoring

- **CloudWatch:** Monitors metrics and logs for infrastructure and applications.
- **X-Ray:** Provides tracing for distributed applications.

Advanced IaC Use Cases for LLMs

1. Multi-Region Deployments

To minimize latency for global users, deploy LLM services across multiple AWS regions using IaC. Terraform's for_each feature can automate this process.

hcl

```
variable "regions" {
  default = ["us-east-1", "eu-west-1"]
}

resource "aws_instance" "example" {
  for_each      = toset(var.regions)
  provider      = aws.example[each.key]
  instance_type = "t2.micro"
  ami           = "ami-0abcdef1234567890"
}
```

2. Autoscaling with Spot Instances

Use AWS Auto Scaling and Spot Instances for cost-efficient scaling of LLM workloads. Define policies in a CloudFormation template or Terraform configuration.

Integrating Other IaC Tools

1. Ansible

Ansible complements Terraform or CloudFormation by automating post-deployment tasks, such as configuring software or deploying models.

Example: Configuring an EC2 Instance

yaml

```yaml
- hosts: all
  tasks:
    - name: Install Python
      yum:
        name: python3
        state: present
    - name: Deploy LLM Model
      copy:
        src: /local/path/model.pt
        dest: /opt/model.pt
```

2. Kubernetes with Helm

For containerized LLM deployments, Kubernetes ensures scalability, while Helm manages application configurations.

Example: Helm Chart for LLM Inference Service

```yaml
apiVersion: v1
kind: Pod
metadata:
  name: llm-inference
spec:
  containers:
  - name: llm-container
    image: llm-inference:latest
    resources:
      limits:
        memory: "4Gi"
        cpu: "2"
```

Best Practices for IaC with LLM Deployments

1. **Use Modular Configurations**
   - Break IaC templates into reusable modules. For example, create separate modules for compute, storage, and networking.

2. **Automate Testing**
   - Use tools like terratest or aws cloudformation validate-template to test IaC templates before applying changes.

3. **Version Control**
   - Store IaC files in repositories like GitHub or GitLab, enabling collaborative development and version tracking.

4. **Implement Security Best Practices**
   - Use AWS IAM roles and policies to enforce the principle of least privilege.
   - Encrypt sensitive data in transit and at rest.

5. **Enable Rollbacks**
   - Use Terraform state management or AWS CloudFormation change sets to roll back to previous infrastructure states if needed.

Case Study: Deploying an LLM-Powered API Using Terraform

Scenario

A fintech company needs to deploy an LLM-powered API for fraud detection, with high availability and low latency.

Solution

1. **Define Infrastructure:**
   - Use Terraform to provision an EC2 Auto Scaling group with GPU instances for inference.
   - Store model weights in S3 and configure secure VPC networking.

2. **Automate Configuration:**
   - Use Ansible to install dependencies, deploy the LLM, and configure monitoring agents on EC2 instances.

3. **Deploy and Test:**
   - Apply Terraform configurations to deploy resources.
   - Validate the deployment with test queries.

4. **Monitor and Scale:**

- Integrate with CloudWatch to monitor API performance and trigger auto-scaling during high traffic.

Conclusion

Infrastructure as Code is a game-changer for deploying LLMs in production environments. By automating the provisioning and management of resources using tools like AWS CloudFormation, Terraform, and Ansible, teams can achieve scalable, reliable, and efficient infrastructure. As the complexity of LLM deployments grows, IaC ensures that infrastructure management remains consistent, cost-effective, and easy to maintain, paving the way for robust AI applications in real-world scenarios.

Continuous Training and Monitoring for Performance

Deploying large language models (LLMs) is only the beginning of their lifecycle. Once in production, these models must be continuously trained and monitored to maintain performance, adapt to changing requirements, and handle evolving datasets. This iterative process ensures that models stay relevant, robust, and aligned with user expectations.

In this chapter, we explore the principles, workflows, and tools necessary for implementing continuous training and monitoring in LLM production environments. The goal is to establish a pipeline that not only maintains model accuracy but also proactively identifies and addresses performance issues.

The Importance of Continuous Training and Monitoring

1. Adapting to Evolving Data

Real-world data is dynamic. Over time, new patterns, terminology, and user preferences emerge, which can render a static model outdated. Continuous training ensures that the model evolves alongside these changes.

2. Mitigating Performance Drift

Performance drift occurs when a model's accuracy degrades over time due to shifts in data distribution. Monitoring and retraining with updated datasets help counteract this drift.

3. Identifying and Correcting Bias

In production, LLMs may exhibit biases that were not apparent during initial testing. Continuous monitoring helps uncover these biases, and retraining on balanced datasets mitigates them.

4. Enhancing Scalability

By automating the retraining and monitoring process, organizations can scale their AI systems to handle increasing data volumes and user interactions without manual intervention.

Principles of Continuous Training

Continuous training is a cyclical process that integrates model retraining into the production workflow. Key principles include:

1. Incremental Learning

Instead of retraining from scratch, incremental learning fine-tunes the model using new data while retaining previous knowledge. This approach reduces computational costs and time.

2. Automated Data Pipeline

A robust data pipeline automates the collection, preprocessing, and labeling of new data. Tools like Apache Airflow or AWS Glue are commonly used for this purpose.

3. Feedback Loop Integration

Incorporating user feedback allows the model to learn from its mistakes. For example, incorrect predictions can be flagged and fed back into the training dataset.

Setting Up Continuous Training

Step 1: Data Collection

Continuous training starts with gathering fresh data. Data sources include:

- User interactions (e.g., chatbot conversations).
- External datasets (e.g., news articles or domain-specific updates).
- Logged errors and user feedback.

Step 2: Data Preprocessing

Preprocessing ensures that data is clean, consistent, and ready for training. Steps include:

- **Tokenization:** Convert raw text into tokens using the model's tokenizer.
- **Filtering:** Remove irrelevant or duplicate data.
- **Augmentation:** Expand datasets with techniques like paraphrasing or back-translation.

```python
from transformers import AutoTokenizer

tokenizer = AutoTokenizer.from_pretrained("gpt2")
def preprocess(data):
    return tokenizer(data, truncation=True, padding=True)
```

Step 3: Dataset Versioning

Versioning datasets ensures traceability and reproducibility. Tools like DVC (Data Version Control) allow you to track dataset changes alongside model updates.

Step 4: Automated Retraining

Automate the retraining process using machine learning pipelines. Frameworks like Kubeflow or SageMaker Pipelines enable end-to-end automation.

python

```python
from sagemaker.workflow.steps import TrainingStep

training_step = TrainingStep(
    name="RetrainModel",
    estimator=estimator,
    inputs=training_inputs
)
```

Step 5: Model Evaluation

Evaluate the retrained model on a validation dataset to ensure it meets performance benchmarks. Common metrics include:

- **Accuracy:** Measures overall correctness.
- **Perplexity:** Assesses how well the model predicts text sequences.
- **BLEU/ROUGE Scores:** Evaluate text generation tasks.

Principles of Continuous Monitoring

Monitoring LLMs in production involves tracking performance metrics, identifying anomalies, and generating actionable insights.

1. Real-Time Metric Collection

Key metrics to monitor include:

- **Latency:** Time taken to generate a response.
- **Throughput:** Number of requests processed per second.
- **Error Rate:** Frequency of incorrect predictions.
- **Resource Utilization:** CPU, GPU, and memory usage.

2. Anomaly Detection

Automated systems can flag anomalies, such as sudden spikes in latency or unexpected drops in accuracy. Tools like AWS CloudWatch or Prometheus are ideal for real-time monitoring.

3. Behavioral Analysis

Monitor how users interact with the model to detect biases, unintended behavior, or gaps in understanding.

4. Drift Detection

Data drift and concept drift occur when the statistical properties of input data change. Drift detection tools, such as Evidently AI, can identify shifts that impact model performance.

Setting Up Continuous Monitoring

Step 1: Logging

Log every interaction the model has with users, including inputs, outputs, and system metrics. Centralized logging systems like Elasticsearch or Fluentd simplify data aggregation.

Step 2: Dashboards

Use visualization tools like Grafana or Tableau to create real-time dashboards that display performance metrics and trends.

Step 3: Alerting

Set up alerts for critical issues, such as model unavailability or performance degradation. Alerting systems like PagerDuty can notify teams via email, SMS, or chat.

Step 4: Regular Audits

Conduct periodic audits to review logged data and identify systemic issues, such as recurring errors or biased predictions.

Combining Training and Monitoring

Continuous training and monitoring are interconnected processes. An efficient system integrates these workflows to form a feedback loop:

1. **Monitor Model Behavior:** Log interactions and track metrics in real time.
2. **Detect Issues:** Identify errors, biases, or drift through automated systems.
3. **Retrain Model:** Use flagged data to update the model, ensuring it adapts to new patterns.
4. **Deploy Updates:** Replace the old model with the retrained version, ensuring minimal downtime.

Tools and Frameworks for Continuous Training and Monitoring

1. MLOps Platforms

MLOps platforms like SageMaker, MLflow, and TFX (TensorFlow Extended) provide integrated solutions for managing the entire machine learning lifecycle.

2. Drift Detection Tools

- **Evidently AI:** Tracks data drift and performance metrics.
- **Alibi Detect:** Detects adversarial attacks, concept drift, and outliers.

3. Monitoring Tools

- **Prometheus:** Collects and queries metrics for infrastructure and applications.
- **Grafana:** Visualizes metrics through customizable dashboards.

4. Orchestration Frameworks

- **Kubeflow:** Automates machine learning workflows in Kubernetes.
- **Airflow:** Schedules and monitors data pipelines.

Challenges in Continuous Training and Monitoring

1. **Data Quality**
   - Poorly labeled or noisy data can degrade model performance. Invest in robust data preprocessing and labeling practices.

2. **Resource Constraints**
   - Continuous training demands significant computational resources. Use cloud-based solutions or hybrid approaches to manage costs.

3. **Model Versioning**
   - Managing multiple model versions can become complex. Use tools like Git for version control and clearly define rollback strategies.

4. **Ethical Considerations**
   - Monitoring systems must safeguard user privacy and comply with regulations like GDPR or CCPA.

Case Study: Continuous Training and Monitoring in E-Commerce

Scenario

An e-commerce platform deploys an LLM-powered recommendation engine to suggest products based on user behavior.

Implementation

1. **Data Pipeline:** Logs user interactions, such as clicks and purchases, in real time.
2. **Drift Detection:** Monitors shifts in product trends and user preferences.
3. **Retraining:** Automatically fine-tunes the model weekly using the latest interaction data.
4. **Monitoring:** Tracks performance metrics like click-through rate (CTR) and conversion rate via dashboards.

Outcome

The platform achieves a 15% increase in CTR and reduces model maintenance costs by 25% through automated workflows.

Best Practices

1. **Start Small:** Begin with simple monitoring and training workflows, then scale as needed.
2. **Automate Everything:** Use automation to reduce manual effort and minimize errors.
3. **Collaborate Across Teams:** Involve data scientists, engineers, and domain experts in the training and monitoring process.
4. **Ensure Transparency:** Maintain detailed logs and documentation to support audits and debugging.

Conclusion

Continuous training and monitoring are indispensable for maintaining the performance and reliability of LLMs in production. By integrating these processes into the deployment workflow, organizations can ensure their models remain accurate, efficient, and aligned with user needs over time. Leveraging the tools and strategies outlined in this chapter, you can build systems that adapt to change, scale seamlessly, and deliver long-term value.

Chapter 10: Optimizing LLMs for Efficiency

Inference Optimization: Speed and Cost Reduction

As large language models (LLMs) are deployed in production environments, inference—the process of generating predictions or outputs from a trained model—often becomes a critical bottleneck. Whether the task involves answering user queries, generating text, or classifying data, optimizing inference is crucial to ensure low latency, high throughput, and cost efficiency. This chapter explores strategies and techniques for optimizing LLM inference, focusing on practical approaches to balance performance and resource utilization.

Why Inference Optimization is Critical

1. Latency Reduction

Users expect real-time responses from AI-powered systems. High latency can degrade user experience, particularly in applications like chatbots, recommendation systems, or search engines.

2. Cost Management

Inference in LLMs requires significant computational resources, especially when dealing with large-scale models. Optimizing inference reduces the operational costs of deploying and maintaining these models.

3. Scalability

Optimized inference allows systems to handle a higher volume of requests without additional hardware, making them more scalable and robust.

Key Components of Inference Optimization

1. Model Size and Complexity

The size and architecture of the model directly impact inference speed and cost. Larger models typically deliver higher accuracy but at the expense of increased computational demands.

2. Hardware Utilization

Efficient utilization of GPUs, TPUs, or CPUs is essential for minimizing latency and maximizing throughput during inference.

3. Batch Processing

Processing multiple requests simultaneously (batching) improves hardware efficiency, particularly for GPU-based inference.

4. Parallelism and Distribution

Distributing inference tasks across multiple devices or nodes enhances system throughput and reduces bottlenecks.

Techniques for Inference Optimization

1. Model Quantization

Quantization reduces the precision of model parameters (e.g., from 32-bit floating-point to 8-bit integers) without significantly affecting accuracy.

Types of Quantization:

- **Post-Training Quantization:** Applied to a trained model without retraining.
- **Quantization-Aware Training:** Incorporates quantization during training for better accuracy preservation.

Example with PyTorch:

```python
import torch
from torch.quantization import quantize_dynamic

model = torch.load("large_model.pth")
quantized_model = quantize_dynamic(model, {torch.nn.Linear}, dtype=torch.qint8)
torch.save(quantized_model, "quantized_model.pth")
```

Benefits:

- Reduces model size.
- Improves inference speed.
- Lowers memory and power consumption.

2. Model Pruning

Pruning removes redundant or less critical parameters from the model, reducing computational requirements while maintaining performance.

Types of Pruning:

- **Structured Pruning:** Removes entire neurons, filters, or layers.
- **Unstructured Pruning:** Eliminates individual weights based on importance.

Implementation:

1. Identify less significant parameters using techniques like weight magnitude.
2. Retrain the model to recover lost accuracy.

Example with TensorFlow:

python

import tensorflow_model_optimization as tfmot

prune_low_magnitude = tfmot.sparsity.keras.prune_low_magnitude

pruned_model = prune_low_magnitude(model)

Benefits:

- Accelerates inference by reducing the number of operations.
- Decreases memory usage.

3. Knowledge Distillation

Knowledge distillation transfers knowledge from a large "teacher" model to a smaller "student" model. The student model mimics the teacher's behavior but is more efficient in terms of speed and size.

Steps:

1. Train a teacher model on the target task.
2. Use the teacher's predictions as soft labels to train the student model.
3. Deploy the smaller student model for inference.

Example:

python

from transformers import DistilBertForSequenceClassification

student_model = DistilBertForSequenceClassification.from_pretrained("distilbert-base-uncased")

student_model.train(teacher_outputs, student_inputs)

Benefits:

- Reduces model size significantly.
- Retains most of the accuracy of the original model.

4. Batch Inference

Batching groups multiple inference requests together, utilizing hardware resources more efficiently and reducing overhead.

Implementation:

- Use frameworks like TensorRT or ONNX Runtime for optimized batch processing.
- Adjust batch size based on available memory and latency requirements.

Example with PyTorch:

python

batch = torch.stack([input1, input2, input3])

outputs = model(batch)

Trade-offs:

- Larger batch sizes improve throughput but may increase latency for individual requests.

5. Offloading and Caching

- **Offloading:** Offload less critical tasks (e.g., preprocessing or simple computations) to lower-cost CPUs, reserving GPUs for model inference.
- **Caching:** Cache frequent queries or results to avoid redundant inference.

Example:

- Use Redis or Memcached to store and retrieve cached outputs for frequently occurring inputs.

6. Model Sharding

For extremely large models that exceed the memory capacity of a single GPU, sharding divides the model across multiple devices.

Implementation:

- Distribute layers of the model across GPUs.
- Use frameworks like PyTorch Distributed or TensorFlow Mesh.

Example:

python

from torch.distributed.pipeline.sync import Pipe

sharded_model = Pipe(model, chunks=2)

Benefits:
- Enables deployment of large models.
- Balances memory and computation across devices.

7. Hardware Acceleration

1. **Using TPUs (Tensor Processing Units):** Specialized hardware for faster inference.
2. **Edge Deployment:** Deploy lightweight models on edge devices using libraries like TensorFlow Lite or ONNX Runtime.

Example with TensorFlow Lite:

```python
import tensorflow as tf

converter = tf.lite.TFLiteConverter.from_saved_model("saved_model")
tflite_model = converter.convert()
with open("model.tflite", "wb") as f:
    f.write(tflite_model)
```

8. Asynchronous Inference

Handle requests asynchronously to improve system throughput and reduce perceived latency.

Example with Python asyncio:

```python
import asyncio

async def infer(request):
    return model(request)

async def main():
    results = await asyncio.gather(infer(request1), infer(request2))
```

Real-World Applications of Inference Optimization

1. Chatbots and Virtual Assistants

- **Challenge:** Deliver real-time responses with minimal latency.
- **Solution:** Use quantization and batching to improve response times while maintaining conversational quality.

2. Content Moderation

- **Challenge:** Process thousands of user-generated posts per second.
- **Solution:** Deploy pruned or distilled models for high-speed classification.

3. Recommendation Systems

- **Challenge:** Provide personalized recommendations for millions of users simultaneously.
- **Solution:** Use sharding and caching to handle high query volumes efficiently.

Tools for Inference Optimization

1. ONNX Runtime

- Supports model optimization and efficient inference for multiple frameworks.
- Offers quantization and hardware-specific optimizations.

2. TensorRT

- NVIDIA's high-performance inference engine for GPU-accelerated applications.
- Provides optimizations for batching, quantization, and layer fusion.

3. Hugging Face Transformers

- Simplifies deployment of optimized transformer models.
- Supports tools like optimum for integrating hardware accelerators.

4. Apache TVM

- Compiles machine learning models for optimal performance on various hardware backends.

Challenges and Trade-offs

1. Accuracy vs. Efficiency

Optimizations like quantization and pruning may reduce model accuracy. Balancing trade-offs is critical for maintaining application quality.

2. Hardware Costs

While GPUs and TPUs improve inference speed, their costs can escalate for large-scale deployments.

3. Complexity

Implementing advanced techniques like model sharding or asynchronous processing increases system complexity, requiring specialized expertise.

Conclusion

Inference optimization is essential for deploying LLMs that are fast, cost-effective, and scalable. By employing techniques such as quantization, pruning, knowledge distillation, and batching, developers can significantly reduce latency and operational expenses without sacrificing performance. As AI-powered applications continue to grow, optimizing inference will remain a cornerstone of successful LLM deployment in production environments.

RAG Pipelines for Real-Time Data Ingestion

Retrieval-Augmented Generation (RAG) is a groundbreaking paradigm that combines large language models (LLMs) with external knowledge retrieval to deliver dynamic, accurate, and contextually relevant responses. Traditional LLMs rely solely on pre-trained parameters, limiting their ability to respond to queries requiring up-to-date or domain-specific information. RAG pipelines overcome this limitation by integrating real-time data ingestion mechanisms, enabling the model to access, process, and utilize fresh information at inference time.

This chapter explores the architecture, benefits, and implementation of RAG pipelines, focusing on their role in real-time data ingestion and practical applications across industries.

Understanding RAG Pipelines

What is RAG?

RAG combines two fundamental processes:

1. **Retrieval:** Identifying relevant external documents or data sources based on a query.
2. **Generation:** Using an LLM to generate responses by synthesizing retrieved data with pre-trained knowledge.

This dual mechanism allows the model to augment its responses with external, real-time information, ensuring relevance and accuracy.

Why Real-Time Data Ingestion is Critical

Real-time data ingestion enables RAG pipelines to:

- Address queries requiring up-to-date information (e.g., news updates, stock prices).
- Incorporate domain-specific knowledge not included in pre-trained models.
- Adapt to dynamic datasets, such as user-generated content or rapidly changing regulatory environments.

RAG Pipeline Architecture

A typical RAG pipeline consists of the following components:

1. Query Preprocessing

- Tokenizes and normalizes user queries to improve retrieval accuracy.
- Applies techniques like stop-word removal and stemming for efficient search.

2. Retriever

- Retrieves relevant documents or data chunks from an external knowledge base.
- Common retrievers:
    - **Sparse Vector Models:** BM25 or TF-IDF.
    - **Dense Vector Models:** Neural retrievers like DPR (Dense Passage Retrieval).

3. Reader (LLM)

- Processes retrieved documents and generates a final response.
- Models like GPT-3 or BERT are commonly used as readers.

4. Real-Time Data Sources

- External knowledge bases, APIs, or streaming data systems serve as sources of fresh data.
- Examples: Elasticsearch indices, SQL databases, or real-time feeds like Kafka.

5. Feedback Loop

- Captures user feedback to improve retrieval accuracy and response quality over time.

Building a RAG Pipeline for Real-Time Data Ingestion

Step 1: Setting Up the Knowledge Base

The knowledge base is the backbone of a RAG pipeline, storing data that can be retrieved at runtime.

1. **Choosing a Storage Solution**
    - **Elasticsearch:** Ideal for full-text search and indexing.
    - **Vector Databases:** Pinecone or Weaviate for dense vector storage.
    - **Relational Databases:** PostgreSQL or MySQL for structured data.
2. **Indexing Data**
    - Structure data into retrievable chunks (e.g., splitting long documents into paragraphs).
    - Generate embeddings for dense retrieval using pre-trained models like Sentence Transformers.

python

from sentence_transformers import SentenceTransformer

model = SentenceTransformer("all-MiniLM-L6-v2")

embeddings = model.encode(document_chunks)

- Store these embeddings in a vector database.

Step 2: Real-Time Data Ingestion

Real-time ingestion ensures that the knowledge base remains current, capturing and indexing new data as it becomes available.

1. **Data Sources**
    - APIs: Ingest data from APIs (e.g., news, weather, stock prices).
    - Streaming Services: Use Kafka or AWS Kinesis for event-driven data ingestion.
    - Web Scraping: Collect data from websites using tools like Scrapy or Beautiful Soup.
2. **Ingestion Frameworks**
    - **Apache Kafka:** A distributed streaming platform for real-time data ingestion.
    - **Apache Flink:** Processes and analyzes streaming data in real-time.

python

from kafka import KafkaConsumer

consumer = KafkaConsumer("real_time_data", bootstrap_servers="localhost:9092")

for message in consumer:

   process_and_store(message.value)

3. **Indexing Pipeline**
    - Preprocess incoming data (e.g., cleaning, tokenizing).
    - Generate embeddings and update the knowledge base.

Step 3: Query Processing and Retrieval

Efficient query processing and retrieval ensure that the pipeline delivers accurate and relevant results in real-time.

1. **Query Preprocessing**
    - Tokenize and vectorize the query using the same embedding model as the knowledge base.

python

Copia codice

```python
query_embedding = model.encode(query)
```

2. **Retriever**
    - Use a hybrid approach combining sparse (BM25) and dense (vector-based) retrieval for optimal results.
    - Perform a nearest-neighbor search in the vector space using tools like FAISS or Pinecone.

python

```python
import faiss

index = faiss.IndexFlatL2(dimension)
index.add(embeddings)
results = index.search(query_embedding, k=5)
```

Step 4: LLM Integration and Response Generation

1. **Combining Retrieval with Generation**
    - Pass the retrieved documents to the LLM as context for response generation.
    - Use prompt engineering to structure the input effectively.

python

Copia codice

```python
context = " ".join(retrieved_documents)
prompt = f"Using the following context, answer the question: {context}\nQuestion: {query}\nAnswer:"
response = llm.generate(prompt)
```

2. **Real-Time Constraints**
    - Optimize LLM inference for low latency using techniques like batching or model quantization.

Optimizing RAG Pipelines for Performance

1. Data Chunking

- Split documents into smaller chunks (e.g., 200-300 words) for precise retrieval.
- Ensure overlap between chunks to preserve context.

2. Embedding Optimization
- Use domain-specific embedding models for better semantic understanding.
- Fine-tune pre-trained models if necessary.

3. Caching
- Cache frequent queries and responses to reduce retrieval and inference overhead.

4. Load Balancing
- Distribute queries across multiple retrievers or LLM instances to prevent bottlenecks.

Applications of RAG Pipelines

1. Customer Support
- Provide accurate, up-to-date responses to user queries by retrieving information from product documentation or FAQs.

2. Legal Research
- Retrieve and analyze case law or regulations in real-time for legal professionals.

3. Financial Analysis
- Combine LLMs with real-time stock market data to generate financial insights and recommendations.

4. Personalized Recommendations
- Retrieve user-specific data from CRM systems to deliver tailored content or suggestions.

Challenges in Real-Time Data Ingestion

1. Latency
Real-time pipelines must balance speed and accuracy, particularly when integrating external APIs or large datasets.

2. Data Quality
Poorly indexed or outdated data can lead to irrelevant or incorrect responses.

3. Scalability
As data and query volumes grow, the system must scale to maintain performance.

4. Security

Ensure that real-time data ingestion complies with privacy regulations (e.g., GDPR, CCPA) and protects sensitive information.

Future Trends in RAG Pipelines

1. Hybrid Retrieval Models

Combining sparse and dense retrieval methods will continue to improve the accuracy and efficiency of RAG pipelines.

2. Adaptive Pipelines

Future systems will dynamically adapt retrieval and generation strategies based on the complexity of the query or available resources.

3. Multimodal Retrieval

Incorporating data beyond text, such as images, audio, or video, will expand the capabilities of RAG pipelines.

Conclusion

RAG pipelines represent a powerful solution for real-time data ingestion, enabling LLMs to provide accurate and contextually enriched responses. By combining advanced retrieval techniques, efficient data ingestion workflows, and scalable infrastructure, RAG systems unlock new possibilities for dynamic, real-world applications. With the strategies outlined in this chapter, you can design RAG pipelines that are not only high-performing but also robust and adaptable to the demands of modern AI-driven systems.

Leveraging Vector Databases and Non-Parametric Knowledge

Large language models (LLMs) have revolutionized artificial intelligence, offering impressive capabilities in text generation, question answering, and semantic search. However, their reliance on pre-trained parameters limits their ability to incorporate real-time or domain-specific knowledge effectively. To address this, LLMs can be enhanced by leveraging **vector databases** and **non-parametric knowledge** systems. These technologies enable dynamic retrieval of information at runtime, bridging the gap between static model training and dynamic, evolving data.

This chapter explores the principles of vector databases and non-parametric knowledge, their applications in enhancing LLMs, and strategies for implementing these systems effectively.

Understanding Vector Databases and Non-Parametric Knowledge

What Are Vector Databases?

Vector databases are specialized systems designed to store, index, and retrieve high-dimensional vector representations of data. These vectors, often embeddings generated by neural networks, capture semantic meaning, allowing for efficient similarity searches.

Key Features:

- **Semantic Search:** Retrieve data based on meaning rather than exact keyword matches.
- **High-Dimensional Indexing:** Use algorithms like Approximate Nearest Neighbors (ANN) to search large datasets efficiently.
- **Scalability:** Handle millions or billions of vector records.

What is Non-Parametric Knowledge?

Non-parametric knowledge refers to external data sources that are not encoded within a model's parameters. Instead, this knowledge is accessed dynamically during inference. Examples include:

- Knowledge bases (e.g., Wikidata, domain-specific corpora).
- Real-time APIs (e.g., weather, financial data).
- Retrieved document chunks stored in vector databases.

Benefits:

- Provides access to up-to-date and specialized knowledge.
- Reduces the need for retraining models with new information.
- Enables customizable, task-specific responses.

How Vector Databases Enhance LLMs

1. Enabling Dynamic Knowledge Retrieval

Vector databases allow LLMs to retrieve and integrate external knowledge dynamically. For instance, a model generating financial reports can query a vector database populated with real-time market data, ensuring responses are both accurate and current.

2. Augmenting Model Outputs

When coupled with a Retrieval-Augmented Generation (RAG) pipeline, vector databases enable LLMs to incorporate retrieved data into their responses, improving relevance and accuracy.

Workflow Example:

1. User inputs a query.
2. Query is embedded into a vector.
3. Vector database retrieves relevant embeddings.
4. LLM generates a response using retrieved data as context.

3. Improving Search Precision

Traditional keyword-based search systems often fail to capture the semantic nuances of queries. Vector databases enable models to perform context-aware retrieval, matching user intents more effectively.

Core Components of a Vector Database System

1. **Embeddings**
    - Represent textual or multimodal data as dense vectors. Common embedding models include:
        - Sentence Transformers (e.g., "all-MiniLM-L6-v2").
        - OpenAI's embedding APIs.
    - Precompute and store embeddings for all documents in the database.

```python
from sentence_transformers import SentenceTransformer

model = SentenceTransformer("all-MiniLM-L6-v2")
embeddings = model.encode(["Document 1", "Document 2"])
```

2. **Indexing**
    - Vector databases use indexing algorithms like **FAISS** or **Annoy** for fast similarity searches.
    - Indexes organize vectors into structures like trees or clusters to enable efficient retrieval.

```python
import faiss

index = faiss.IndexFlatL2(embedding_dimension)
index.add(embeddings)
```

3. **Similarity Metrics**
    - Measure the distance or similarity between vectors using metrics like:
        - **Cosine Similarity**
        - **Euclidean Distance**
        - **Dot Product**

4. **Integration with LLMs**
    - Combine retrieved vectors with LLM prompts for context-aware generation.

Key Tools for Vector Databases

1. **Pinecone**
    - A fully managed vector database with built-in scaling and support for real-time search.
    - Integrates seamlessly with LLM frameworks.

python

```
import pinecone

pinecone.init(api_key="your-api-key", environment="us-west1-gcp")
index = pinecone.Index("example-index")
index.upsert([("id1", embedding1), ("id2", embedding2)])
```

2. **Weaviate**
    - Open-source vector database with native support for semantic search and data schemas.
    - Includes integrations with huggingface and OpenAI models.

3. **FAISS**
    - An open-source library developed by Facebook for efficient vector indexing and similarity search.
    - Suitable for custom deployments with large-scale datasets.

4. **Milvus**
    - A cloud-native, open-source vector database optimized for AI applications.
    - Supports integrations with TensorFlow, PyTorch, and Kubernetes.

Non-Parametric Knowledge Integration

1. Data Sources

Non-parametric knowledge is derived from a variety of sources:

- **Structured Databases:** Relational databases like PostgreSQL for tabular data.
- **Document Repositories:** Collections of documents, articles, or PDFs.
- **Real-Time APIs:** APIs for live data, such as stock market updates or news feeds.

2. Querying Non-Parametric Knowledge

Dynamic queries enable the retrieval of the most relevant information from external sources. For instance:

- **SQL Queries:** Retrieve structured data.

- **RESTful APIs:** Fetch real-time information.

```python
import requests

response = requests.get("https://api.example.com/data")
retrieved_data = response.json()
```

3. Combining with LLMs

Use the retrieved non-parametric knowledge as context for generating responses. This approach minimizes hallucinations and improves factual accuracy.

Applications of Vector Databases and Non-Parametric Knowledge

1. Customer Support
- Retrieve product manuals or FAQs dynamically to generate precise, helpful responses.

2. Healthcare
- Access medical databases to provide evidence-based recommendations.

3. Legal Research
- Query legal precedents and case law for accurate insights.

4. Personalized Recommendations
- Leverage user profiles stored as embeddings to deliver tailored suggestions.

Optimizing Vector Database Performance

1. Efficient Indexing
- Use hierarchical or partitioned indexes to improve search latency on large datasets.

2. Batch Processing
- Process and index large datasets in parallel to reduce ingestion time.

3. Hardware Acceleration
- Leverage GPUs for embedding generation and vector similarity computations.

4. Incremental Updates
- Enable real-time updates to keep the database current without rebuilding the index.

Challenges in Leveraging Vector Databases and Non-Parametric Knowledge

1. Scalability

As datasets grow, maintaining low-latency searches requires advanced indexing and distributed systems.

2. Data Quality

Poor-quality or noisy data can lead to irrelevant or incorrect retrievals.

3. Integration Complexity

Integrating vector databases with LLMs and other tools requires careful engineering to ensure compatibility and performance.

4. Cost

Storing and querying high-dimensional embeddings at scale can be resource-intensive.

Future Directions

1. **Multimodal Retrieval** Vector databases will increasingly support embeddings for text, images, and audio, enabling richer retrieval capabilities.
2. **Federated Search** Combine multiple data sources and retrieval mechanisms into a unified system for comprehensive knowledge access.
3. **Automated Index Optimization** AI-driven optimization of indexing strategies will reduce latency and improve scalability.

Conclusion

Vector databases and non-parametric knowledge systems are essential tools for enhancing the capabilities of large language models. By enabling dynamic retrieval of external information, these technologies ensure that LLMs remain accurate, relevant, and adaptable to evolving data landscapes. Through careful integration, indexing, and optimization, developers can unlock the full potential of these systems, creating powerful AI applications that combine the strengths of pre-trained models with real-time, domain-specific knowledge.

Part 5: Advanced Topics and Innovations

Chapter 11: Beyond Text: Building Multimodal Applications

Integrating Vision, Audio, and Text Models

The next frontier of artificial intelligence lies in building multimodal applications that seamlessly integrate vision, audio, and text models. Multimodal AI aims to mimic the human ability to process and understand information across different sensory inputs, enabling machines to generate richer, more context-aware outputs. By combining these modalities, developers can create advanced applications ranging from conversational agents capable of analyzing visual context to assistive technologies for individuals with disabilities.

This chapter delves into the principles, challenges, and methodologies for integrating vision, audio, and text models, highlighting their transformative potential and real-world applications.

Why Multimodal Integration Matters

1. Enhanced Understanding

Text alone often lacks the full context required for accurate comprehension. For example:

- Describing a scene ("a beach with a red umbrella") is far less powerful than pairing it with an image.
- Understanding spoken text can be enriched by visual cues, such as facial expressions or gestures.

2. Broader Applicability

Integrating vision, audio, and text expands the range of use cases, including:

- Video captioning: Generating text descriptions of visual content.
- Multimodal search: Enabling users to query data using combinations of images, audio, and text.
- Virtual assistants: Interpreting spoken commands in the context of visual data.

3. Improved Accessibility

Multimodal systems can bridge communication gaps, such as transcribing spoken words for the hearing impaired or describing visual scenes for the visually impaired.

Components of a Multimodal System

A robust multimodal system consists of the following components:

1. Vision Models

Vision models process and analyze visual data, such as images or videos. Examples include:

- **Convolutional Neural Networks (CNNs):** For tasks like object detection and image classification.
- **Vision Transformers (ViTs):** Advanced architectures that use attention mechanisms for superior performance on visual tasks.

2. Audio Models

Audio models handle sound data, including speech and environmental sounds. Examples include:

- **Recurrent Neural Networks (RNNs) and Transformers:** For speech recognition and audio classification.
- **WaveNet or MelGAN:** For audio generation tasks.

3. Text Models

Text models process and generate natural language. LLMs like GPT-3 and BERT excel in text-based tasks, from summarization to question answering.

4. Fusion Mechanism

Combining outputs from different modalities is critical for multimodal systems. Fusion can occur at:

- **Early Fusion:** Merging raw data from different modalities.
- **Intermediate Fusion:** Combining encoded features from each modality.
- **Late Fusion:** Integrating predictions or outputs from individual models.

Techniques for Integrating Vision, Audio, and Text

1. Unified Architectures

Unified architectures process multiple modalities within a single model. For example:

- **CLIP (Contrastive Language–Image Pretraining):** Aligns images with text by training on paired data, enabling tasks like image captioning and visual search.
- **FLAVA (Foundational Language and Vision Alignment):** A general-purpose model for both vision and language tasks.

Example: Using CLIP for Text-Image Matching

python

from transformers import CLIPProcessor, CLIPModel

model = CLIPModel.from_pretrained("openai/clip-vit-base-patch32")

processor = CLIPProcessor.from_pretrained("openai/clip-vit-base-patch32")

inputs = processor(text=["A dog playing fetch"], images=image, return_tensors="pt")

```
outputs = model(**inputs)

logits_per_image = outputs.logits_per_image
```

2. Cross-Modal Attention

Cross-modal attention mechanisms allow models to focus on relevant parts of the input from different modalities. For instance:

- In video captioning, attention can align audio cues with specific video frames to generate accurate text descriptions.
- In speech-to-text applications, attention helps synchronize spoken words with contextual visual elements.

3. Embedding Alignment

Embedding alignment ensures that representations from different modalities exist in the same latent space. This allows meaningful comparisons and interactions across modalities.

- **Text-to-Image Alignment:** Aligning word embeddings with visual embeddings (e.g., mapping "dog" to its visual counterpart).
- **Audio-to-Text Alignment:** Aligning spectrogram representations with text embeddings for speech recognition.

4. Multimodal Transformers

Multimodal transformers extend the transformer architecture to handle inputs from multiple modalities. These models often include modality-specific encoders and a shared cross-modal encoder.

Example: Multimodal Transformer Workflow

1. Encode text, images, and audio separately.
2. Pass encoded features through a cross-modal transformer for fusion.
3. Decode fused features for the final output.

Building a Multimodal Application

Example: Multimodal Video Captioning

A video captioning system generates text descriptions for videos by integrating vision, audio, and text models.

Step 1: Preprocessing

- Extract frames from the video using OpenCV.
- Convert audio into spectrograms using libraries like Librosa.

Step 2: Feature Extraction

- Use a vision model (e.g., ViT) to extract features from frames.
- Process audio spectrograms with an audio model (e.g., Wav2Vec2).
- Generate text embeddings using a language model (e.g., BERT).

Step 3: Fusion

- Concatenate features from all modalities.
- Pass them through a multimodal transformer for fusion and context-aware representation.

Step 4: Text Generation

- Decode fused features into text using an autoregressive decoder (e.g., GPT-2).

Challenges in Multimodal Integration

1. Data Alignment

Aligning data from different modalities can be complex, especially when they have varying temporal resolutions (e.g., synchronizing audio with video frames).

Solution:

- Use temporal alignment techniques, such as dynamic time warping or cross-modal attention.

2. Model Complexity

Multimodal systems often require multiple large models, increasing computational demands and latency.

Solution:

- Use lightweight architectures or model distillation to reduce complexity.

3. Data Scarcity

Multimodal datasets are often smaller and less diverse than unimodal datasets.

Solution:

- Employ data augmentation techniques, such as generating synthetic samples or augmenting individual modalities.

4. Modality-Specific Noise

Each modality may introduce unique noise (e.g., blurry images, background audio).

Solution:

- Preprocess inputs to reduce noise and improve data quality.

Applications of Multimodal Systems

1. Healthcare

- Combining visual data (e.g., X-rays) with patient records (text) and audio data (doctor's notes) for diagnostics.

2. Autonomous Vehicles

- Integrating camera feeds, LIDAR data, and spoken instructions for safe navigation.

3. Content Creation

- Generating rich media content, such as animated videos, based on text or audio prompts.

4. Virtual Assistants

- Enhancing virtual assistants to understand and respond to spoken commands in the context of visual scenes.

Tools and Frameworks for Multimodal Applications

1. **OpenAI CLIP**
   - Aligns text and images for tasks like visual search and image captioning.

2. **Hugging Face Transformers**
   - Offers multimodal transformers like FLAVA and image-text models.

3. **Librosa**
   - Processes audio data, including feature extraction and spectrogram generation.

4. **OpenCV**
   - Handles image and video preprocessing tasks.

5. **Deep Multimodal Learning Frameworks**
   - Libraries like MMF (MultiModal Framework) provide prebuilt modules for integrating multiple modalities.

Future Directions

1. Generalist Models

Future models will handle multiple modalities seamlessly within a single architecture, reducing complexity and enhancing performance.

2. Real-Time Multimodal Applications

As hardware advances, real-time multimodal systems will become more feasible, enabling instant analysis and response across modalities.

3. Multimodal Personalization

AI systems will adapt to individual user preferences and behaviors by integrating multimodal data from personal devices.

Conclusion

Integrating vision, audio, and text models is transforming the AI landscape, enabling richer, more versatile applications that mirror human sensory processing. By leveraging unified architectures, cross-modal attention, and advanced embedding techniques, developers can build systems that excel in diverse real-world tasks. As multimodal AI continues to evolve, its potential to enhance accessibility, creativity, and intelligence remains boundless.

The Emergence of Foundation Models (LFMs)

Foundation models, often referred to as **Large Foundation Models (LFMs)**, represent a transformative leap in the field of artificial intelligence. These models, characterized by their massive scale, multimodal capabilities, and general-purpose nature, have redefined how AI systems are built, deployed, and scaled. Unlike task-specific models, LFMs are pre-trained on extensive datasets and can be fine-tuned or adapted to a wide array of downstream applications. Their emergence has sparked a paradigm shift in AI development, with profound implications across industries.

This chapter explores the rise of LFMs, their architecture, applications, and the challenges and opportunities they present in shaping the future of AI.

What Are Foundation Models?

Foundation models are large-scale, pre-trained AI models designed to serve as a base for a wide range of tasks. They are trained on diverse, massive datasets—often spanning text, images, audio, and other modalities—allowing them to generalize across domains.

Key Characteristics of Foundation Models

1. **Scale**
   - LFMs boast billions or even trillions of parameters, enabling them to capture intricate patterns and relationships in data. For instance:
     - GPT-3 has 175 billion parameters.
     - PaLM (Pathways Language Model) by Google contains 540 billion parameters.

2. **Pretraining**
   - LFMs are pre-trained on diverse datasets using self-supervised learning techniques. This allows them to learn generalized representations of data, which can be fine-tuned for specific tasks.

3. **Multimodal Capabilities**

- Many LFMs can process and generate outputs across multiple modalities, such as text, images, and audio. Examples include OpenAI's **DALL·E** and Google's **MUM (Multitask Unified Model)**.

4. **Versatility**
    - LFMs can perform a wide range of tasks, from natural language understanding to image recognition, without task-specific architectures.

5. **Transferability**
    - Fine-tuning or prompting can adapt LFMs to specialized applications, significantly reducing the need for task-specific training from scratch.

How LFMs Differ from Traditional Models

Traditional AI models are typically designed for narrow tasks, requiring separate models for text classification, image recognition, or speech synthesis. In contrast, LFMs offer a unified approach:

Aspect	Traditional Models	Foundation Models
Scope	Task-specific	General-purpose
Training Data	Narrow and domain-specific	Diverse and large-scale
Fine-Tuning	Mandatory	Optional (prompting is enough)
Multimodal Support	Limited	Native or extensible
Deployment	One model per task	Single model for multiple tasks

Architectural Innovations in LFMs

Foundation models derive their power from advanced architectures and training methodologies:

1. Transformers

Transformers are the cornerstone of LFMs. They use attention mechanisms to process sequences of data, making them highly effective for tasks like text generation and image understanding.

- **Key Components:**
    - **Self-Attention:** Captures relationships between input tokens.
    - **Feedforward Layers:** Encodes contextual information.
    - **Positional Encoding:** Preserves input order for sequence data.
- **Variants:**
    - **Encoder-Only Models:** Optimized for understanding tasks (e.g., BERT).

- **Decoder-Only Models:** Optimized for generation tasks (e.g., GPT-3).
- **Encoder-Decoder Models:** Support both understanding and generation (e.g., T5).

2. Multimodal Architectures

Many LFMs extend the transformer architecture to handle multimodal inputs. For instance:

- **CLIP (Contrastive Language–Image Pretraining):** Aligns image and text embeddings.
- **Flamingo:** Integrates vision and language for tasks like video captioning.

3. Sparse Attention

To manage computational costs, some LFMs adopt sparse attention mechanisms, which focus computation on the most relevant parts of the input.

Applications of Foundation Models

LFMs have unlocked new possibilities across industries, enabling applications that were previously infeasible or prohibitively expensive.

1. Natural Language Processing (NLP)

- **Chatbots and Virtual Assistants:** OpenAI's GPT-4 powers conversational AI systems like ChatGPT, offering context-aware and human-like responses.
- **Text Summarization:** LFMs can condense large volumes of text into concise summaries, aiding fields like journalism and legal analysis.

2. Computer Vision

- **Image Generation:** Models like DALL·E generate high-quality images from textual descriptions, enabling creative design and prototyping.
- **Visual Search:** Google's MUM enhances search by combining text and image inputs, improving context-aware recommendations.

3. Multimodal Applications

- **Medical Diagnostics:** LFMs analyze radiology images alongside patient notes to provide comprehensive insights.
- **Autonomous Vehicles:** Integrating sensor data (e.g., LIDAR) with visual and textual cues enables more accurate decision-making.

4. Scientific Research

- **Drug Discovery:** LFMs process complex datasets, such as protein structures and chemical properties, to accelerate drug discovery.
- **Climate Modeling:** Analyze and predict climate patterns using multimodal data, including satellite images and textual reports.

5. Accessibility

- **Assistive Technologies:** LFMs power tools for real-time transcription, translation, and scene description, improving accessibility for individuals with disabilities.

Challenges in Building and Deploying LFMs

While LFMs are transformative, their development and deployment pose significant challenges:

1. Computational Demands

Training LFMs requires enormous computational resources, including specialized hardware like GPUs or TPUs. For example:

- GPT-3's training reportedly consumed hundreds of petaflop-days of computation.

Solutions:

- Use model distillation to create smaller, efficient versions.
- Collaborate with cloud providers offering high-performance compute environments.

2. Data Bias

LFMs inherit biases present in their training data, leading to problematic outputs in sensitive applications.

Solutions:

- Employ data curation to minimize bias.
- Implement fairness-aware training techniques.

3. Interpretability

The "black-box" nature of LFMs makes it difficult to understand their decision-making processes.

Solutions:

- Use explainability techniques like SHAP or attention visualization.
- Develop tools for auditing and monitoring model behavior.

4. Cost

The financial cost of training and deploying LFMs is prohibitive for many organizations.

Solutions:

- Adopt pre-trained LFMs through open platforms like Hugging Face.
- Leverage transfer learning to reduce fine-tuning costs.

Ethical Considerations

The power of LFMs comes with significant ethical responsibilities:

1. Misinformation

LFMs can generate realistic but false content, raising concerns about misinformation and deepfakes.

Mitigation:

- Implement safeguards to detect and block harmful outputs.
- Establish guidelines for responsible AI usage.

2. Privacy

Processing sensitive data with LFMs may infringe on user privacy.

Mitigation:

- Use differential privacy techniques to anonymize data.
- Follow regulatory frameworks like GDPR and CCPA.

3. Job Displacement

The automation enabled by LFMs could displace human workers in some sectors.

Mitigation:

- Focus on augmenting rather than replacing human capabilities.
- Invest in reskilling programs for affected workers.

Future Directions

1. Personalized LFMs

Future LFMs will adapt to individual users, providing personalized responses and recommendations based on their preferences and history.

2. Efficient Training Paradigms

Advances in techniques like sparsity, low-rank adaptation, and federated learning will reduce the cost and environmental impact of training LFMs.

3. Cross-Language and Multimodal Mastery

Next-generation LFMs will achieve seamless cross-language and multimodal fluency, enabling universal communication and comprehension.

4. Integration with IoT

LFMs will power edge devices, bringing intelligent capabilities to the Internet of Things (IoT) ecosystem.

Conclusion

The emergence of foundation models marks a pivotal moment in the evolution of artificial intelligence. With their unparalleled versatility, scale, and multimodal capabilities, LFMs are reshaping industries and redefining what is possible in AI. However, their development and deployment come with significant challenges that require careful consideration and innovation. As we continue to refine these models, their potential to drive progress and solve complex problems across domains remains boundless.

Chapter 12: Emerging Trends in LLMs

The Future of AI with LLMs

The future of artificial intelligence (AI) is inextricably linked to the evolution of large language models (LLMs). As foundational technologies that drive natural language processing, computer vision, multimodal systems, and even complex decision-making, LLMs are poised to revolutionize industries, redefine human-machine interaction, and address some of society's most pressing challenges. However, this promising future also demands innovative solutions to overcome existing limitations, balance ethical considerations, and harness these technologies responsibly.

This chapter explores the future of AI through the lens of LLMs, focusing on anticipated advancements, transformative applications, and the critical role they will play in shaping a smarter, more interconnected world.

1. Expanding the Frontiers of LLM Capabilities

A. Moving Beyond Text

While LLMs have traditionally excelled in text-based tasks, their scope is rapidly expanding to include multimodal capabilities. Future LLMs will seamlessly integrate text, images, audio, and even video, creating a unified framework for processing diverse data types.

- **Example Applications:**
    - Real-time video analysis combined with natural language summaries.
    - Multimodal virtual assistants capable of interpreting spoken instructions and visual context.
    - Automated content creation tools that generate videos, graphics, and accompanying text narratives.

B. Dynamic Knowledge Integration

The next generation of LLMs will incorporate real-time knowledge retrieval to stay updated with the latest information. Retrieval-Augmented Generation (RAG) systems will become more sophisticated, enabling LLMs to respond accurately to dynamic queries without the need for retraining.

- **Future Features:**
    - Direct integration with APIs for real-time data ingestion.
    - Seamless updates from domain-specific knowledge bases or live data streams.

C. Reasoning and Planning

Current LLMs, while adept at generating coherent text, often struggle with complex reasoning and planning tasks. The future will see LLMs augmented with symbolic reasoning capabilities, enabling them to:

- Solve multi-step problems.
- Simulate decision-making processes.
- Assist in strategic planning across industries like logistics, healthcare, and urban development.

2. Transformative Applications Across Industries

A. Personalized Education

LLMs will redefine education by delivering personalized learning experiences tailored to individual needs. With the ability to:

- Create custom lesson plans.
- Provide real-time tutoring in multiple languages.
- Assess progress and adapt teaching methods dynamically, LLMs can democratize access to high-quality education worldwide.

B. Healthcare Innovation

In healthcare, LLMs will become indispensable tools for diagnostics, treatment planning, and patient care. They will:

- Analyze multimodal patient data, including medical records, imaging, and real-time sensor data from wearable devices.
- Generate actionable insights for clinicians.
- Provide conversational AI interfaces for patient education and support.

C. Creative Industries

LLMs will continue to disrupt creative fields, enabling:

- AI-generated scripts, novels, and music compositions.
- Real-time collaboration between human creators and AI tools.
- Personalized content tailored to audience preferences.

D. Automation and Workforce Transformation

LLMs will drive automation across sectors, from manufacturing and logistics to customer service and financial analysis. Their ability to process vast amounts of unstructured data will enable more informed decision-making and optimize workflows.

3. The Role of LLMs in Shaping Human-AI Collaboration

A. Enhancing Productivity

LLMs will serve as collaborative tools that augment human intelligence, handling repetitive tasks while empowering users to focus on strategic and creative endeavors.

- **Examples:**
    - Drafting legal documents or summarizing contracts for lawyers.
    - Assisting scientists in literature reviews and hypothesis generation.

B. Bridging Communication Gaps

With advanced multilingual capabilities, LLMs will facilitate cross-cultural communication in globalized contexts. They will:

- Translate languages with near-perfect accuracy.
- Act as real-time interpreters in international business or diplomacy.

C. Ethical AI Assistants

As ethical considerations take center stage, LLMs will be designed to:

- Explain their reasoning transparently.
- Provide disclaimers and limitations for their outputs.
- Encourage critical thinking rather than blind reliance on their recommendations.

4. Technological Innovations Driving the Future of LLMs

A. Efficiency at Scale

As LLMs grow in size and capability, managing their computational demands will require significant innovations in efficiency.

- **Sparse Models:** Selectively activate only the necessary parts of a model for specific tasks, reducing computation.
- **Parameter-Efficient Fine-Tuning (PEFT):** Adapt large models for new tasks with minimal additional training.
- **Edge Deployments:** Miniaturized LLMs capable of running on edge devices will reduce reliance on cloud infrastructure.

B. Federated Learning

Decentralized training frameworks will allow LLMs to learn collaboratively across distributed data sources while preserving privacy. This will be especially impactful in industries like healthcare and finance, where data sensitivity is paramount.

C. Advanced Prompt Engineering

Future prompt engineering techniques will focus on:

- Context-aware prompting for complex tasks.
- Hierarchical prompting to break down large problems into manageable sub-tasks.

5. Ethical Considerations for the Future of LLMs

A. Mitigating Bias

Bias in LLMs remains a critical issue, as these models often reflect the biases inherent in their training data. Addressing this will involve:

- Transparent documentation of training datasets.
- Regular audits and updates to mitigate bias over time.
- Incorporating fairness-aware algorithms.

B. Privacy and Security

The widespread adoption of LLMs raises concerns about data privacy and security. Future models will integrate:

- Differential privacy techniques to anonymize sensitive data.
- Robust encryption for secure communication and storage.

C. Preventing Misuse

The powerful capabilities of LLMs also pose risks of misuse, such as generating deepfakes or automating malicious activities. Regulatory frameworks and technical safeguards will be critical to ensure responsible use.

6. Democratizing Access to LLMs

As the power of LLMs becomes increasingly apparent, democratizing access will be essential to ensure equitable benefits. This will involve:

- Open-source initiatives to make LLMs available to researchers and small businesses.
- Educational programs to teach users how to deploy and interact with LLMs effectively.
- Infrastructure subsidies for low-resource regions to enable access to AI technologies.

7. Potential Challenges on the Horizon

A. Environmental Impact

Training and deploying LLMs at scale require significant energy consumption, raising concerns about their environmental footprint. The future will see increased adoption of:

- Renewable energy sources for data centers.
- Energy-efficient architectures like sparsity and quantization.

B. Regulatory Complexity

As LLMs impact sensitive areas like healthcare, finance, and governance, regulatory frameworks will need to evolve to address accountability, transparency, and fairness.

C. Ensuring Human-Centric Design

While LLMs can automate many tasks, maintaining a human-centric approach will be critical to ensure that AI serves as a complement to, rather than a replacement for, human capabilities.

8. Envisioning the Future

Imagine a world where LLMs seamlessly integrate into daily life, powering tools that understand context, anticipate needs, and foster creativity. For example:

- A student in a remote village uses a multimodal assistant to learn science through interactive videos and real-time feedback.
- A doctor collaborates with an AI-powered diagnostic system to identify rare diseases more accurately.
- A company leverages an LLM-driven system to optimize global supply chains, reducing waste and costs.

These scenarios illustrate the transformative potential of LLMs when applied thoughtfully and responsibly.

Conclusion

The future of AI with LLMs is bright, promising transformative advancements across industries and applications. As these models evolve, they will unlock new opportunities for innovation, collaboration, and problem-solving, fundamentally reshaping the way we interact with technology. However, realizing this potential requires addressing critical challenges, fostering ethical practices, and ensuring that the benefits of LLMs are accessible to all. By balancing ambition with responsibility, we can harness the power of LLMs to create a smarter, more equitable, and interconnected world.

Ethical AI: Challenges and Solutions

As large language models (LLMs) redefine the capabilities of artificial intelligence, ethical considerations have become central to their development and deployment. While LLMs hold immense promise, they also pose significant ethical challenges, including bias, misinformation, privacy risks, and the potential for misuse. These challenges demand proactive, innovative solutions to ensure that AI systems align with societal values, respect human rights, and promote fairness.

This chapter examines the ethical dilemmas associated with LLMs, explores their underlying causes, and outlines practical strategies to address these issues. By adopting an ethical approach, developers and organizations can harness the transformative potential of LLMs responsibly.

Key Ethical Challenges in LLMs

1. Bias and Discrimination

One of the most persistent issues with LLMs is bias. These models learn patterns from training data, which often contain societal biases, stereotypes, and historical inequalities. As a result, LLMs can inadvertently perpetuate or amplify these biases in their outputs.

- **Examples of Bias:**
    - Gender Bias: Reinforcing stereotypes, such as associating specific professions with particular genders.
    - Racial Bias: Providing inaccurate or harmful responses related to race or ethnicity.
    - Cultural Bias: Favoring Western perspectives in global or multicultural contexts.
- **Impacts:**
    - Discrimination in decision-making processes, such as hiring or lending.
    - Alienation of marginalized communities.

2. Misinformation and Hallucinations

LLMs can generate text that appears confident and plausible but is factually incorrect or misleading. This phenomenon, known as "hallucination," poses significant risks when LLMs are used in applications like education, journalism, or healthcare.

- **Examples:**
    - Generating fake news articles that mimic credible sources.
    - Providing incorrect medical advice or diagnoses.
- **Impacts:**
    - Erosion of public trust in AI systems.
    - Spread of misinformation on critical topics.

3. Privacy and Data Security

LLMs often rely on vast amounts of data for training, some of which may include sensitive or personal information. The improper use of such data can lead to privacy violations.

- **Examples:**
    - Unintentionally revealing private information during inference.
    - Storing sensitive data without proper anonymization.
- **Impacts:**
    - Non-compliance with data protection regulations (e.g., GDPR, CCPA).
    - Loss of user trust and potential legal repercussions.

4. Misuse and Malicious Applications

The versatility of LLMs makes them susceptible to misuse in harmful ways, such as:

- Generating phishing emails or social engineering scripts.
- Creating deepfakes or propaganda.
- Automating the spread of hate speech or cyberattacks.
- **Impacts:**
    - Threats to cybersecurity.
    - Amplification of harmful content.

5. Lack of Accountability

AI systems, including LLMs, often operate as "black boxes," making it difficult to understand how they arrive at their decisions or outputs. This lack of transparency hinders accountability.

- **Examples:**
    - Difficulty tracing errors in AI-driven decision-making.
    - Inability to explain or justify model predictions.
- **Impacts:**
    - Reduced trust in AI systems.
    - Challenges in auditing and governance.

Addressing Ethical Challenges: Solutions and Best Practices

1. Mitigating Bias

Eliminating bias requires addressing the issue at multiple stages of the AI lifecycle.

- **Data Curation:**
    - Carefully curate and preprocess training data to minimize biases.
    - Use diverse and representative datasets to ensure inclusivity.
- **Algorithmic Fairness:**
    - Implement fairness-aware training techniques, such as reweighting or debiasing algorithms.
    - Regularly audit model outputs for bias using fairness metrics.
- **Human Oversight:**
    - Involve domain experts and diverse stakeholders in model evaluation.
    - Incorporate feedback loops to identify and correct biased outputs.

Example Initiative:

- OpenAI's efforts to refine GPT models include fine-tuning processes and user feedback to reduce bias in generated outputs.

2. Combating Misinformation

To tackle hallucinations and misinformation, LLMs must be equipped with mechanisms for truth verification and reliability.

- **Knowledge Verification:**
    - Integrate Retrieval-Augmented Generation (RAG) pipelines to provide context from trusted external sources during inference.
    - Cross-reference model outputs with verified datasets.
- **User Warnings:**
    - Clearly indicate the limitations of the model, emphasizing that outputs may require fact-checking.
    - Use disclaimers in sensitive domains, such as healthcare or law.
- **Evaluation Frameworks:**
    - Develop standardized evaluation metrics to assess factual accuracy and reliability.

Example Implementation:

- Tools like Google's MUM (Multitask Unified Model) validate responses by drawing from authoritative sources.

3. Ensuring Privacy and Data Security

Data privacy and security can be strengthened through technical safeguards and ethical data practices.

- **Differential Privacy:**
    - Implement techniques that add noise to training data, preserving privacy while maintaining model accuracy.
- **Federated Learning:**
    - Train models locally on user devices, reducing the need to centralize sensitive data.
- **Data Anonymization:**
    - Remove personally identifiable information (PII) from datasets before training.
- **Compliance and Governance:**

- Align with legal frameworks like GDPR and CCPA to ensure ethical data handling.

Example Tool:

- TensorFlow Privacy offers built-in mechanisms to incorporate differential privacy into machine learning workflows.

4. Preventing Misuse

To counter malicious applications, proactive monitoring and safeguards are essential.

- **Access Controls:**
    - Restrict access to high-capability models through authentication or tiered APIs.
    - Implement usage policies and monitor compliance.
- **Content Moderation:**
    - Develop filters to detect and block harmful or abusive content.
    - Employ adversarial testing to anticipate and mitigate misuse scenarios.
- **Ethical Guidelines:**
    - Publish clear guidelines for responsible use of LLMs, backed by enforcement mechanisms.

Example Framework:

- OpenAI's API includes content moderation tools and monitoring systems to detect abuse.

5. Enhancing Transparency and Accountability

Building trust in LLMs requires greater transparency and accountability in their design and deployment.

- **Model Explainability:**
    - Incorporate interpretable AI techniques, such as attention visualization or counterfactual reasoning.
    - Provide clear documentation on model behavior and limitations.
- **Auditing and Governance:**
    - Establish independent auditing mechanisms to evaluate model performance and compliance.
    - Maintain detailed logs for traceability and error analysis.
- **User Empowerment:**
    - Enable users to flag problematic outputs and provide feedback for improvement.
    - Educate users on how to critically evaluate AI-generated content.

Example Initiative:

- Microsoft's Responsible AI Standard outlines principles for transparency, accountability, and fairness in AI systems.

Collaborative Efforts in Ethical AI

1. Multi-Stakeholder Engagement

Collaboration between governments, academia, industry, and civil society is vital for shaping ethical AI practices. By bringing diverse perspectives to the table, stakeholders can address complex challenges more effectively.

- **Examples:**
    - The Partnership on AI, a consortium that includes AI leaders like Google, Microsoft, and IBM, focuses on responsible AI development.
    - UNESCO's AI Ethics Recommendation promotes global consensus on ethical AI principles.

2. Open-Source Contributions

Open-source communities play a critical role in advancing ethical AI by sharing tools, frameworks, and best practices.

- **Examples:**
    - Hugging Face offers open-access models with detailed documentation on ethical considerations.
    - AI Fairness 360, an open-source toolkit, helps developers evaluate and mitigate bias.

3. Policy and Regulation

Policymakers are increasingly introducing regulations to ensure ethical AI deployment.

- **Examples:**
    - The European Union's AI Act establishes guidelines for high-risk AI applications.
    - The US National Institute of Standards and Technology (NIST) is developing a framework for AI risk management.

Looking Ahead: The Path to Ethical AI

The future of ethical AI lies in proactive innovation and collaboration. Developers must embed ethical considerations into the core of AI design, ensuring that LLMs empower society without harm. At the same time, organizations and policymakers must remain vigilant, adapting to emerging challenges and fostering a culture of responsibility.

By addressing bias, misinformation, privacy, misuse, and accountability, the AI community can create systems that reflect humanity's highest ideals—tools that not only solve problems but also uphold trust, equity, and inclusivity.

In navigating the ethical complexities of LLMs, we lay the groundwork for AI technologies that truly serve humanity, ensuring that progress aligns with our shared values and aspirations.

Innovations on the Horizon

The field of large language models (LLMs) is evolving at an unprecedented pace, with groundbreaking innovations poised to redefine the capabilities of artificial intelligence (AI). From advancements in architecture to more efficient deployment strategies, the horizon is rich with possibilities that will extend LLMs beyond their current boundaries. These innovations are not only technical but also practical, addressing challenges like energy consumption, bias, and scalability while enabling entirely new applications across diverse industries.

In this chapter, we delve into the emerging innovations shaping the future of LLMs, examining their implications for technology, business, and society.

1. Next-Generation Architectures

A. Sparse Models for Efficiency

The exponential growth in model size has brought immense computational demands, spurring research into sparse architectures. Unlike dense models, which activate all parameters for every input, sparse models selectively activate only the most relevant portions of the network.

- **Key Innovations:**
    - **Mixture-of-Experts (MoE):** A sparse model architecture where subsets of the model are activated based on input data. MoE systems achieve comparable accuracy to dense models while significantly reducing computational overhead.
    - **Dynamic Routing:** Mechanisms that direct data through the most relevant model paths, optimizing both performance and efficiency.
- **Impact:** Sparse models will allow organizations to deploy high-performance LLMs at lower costs, democratizing access to cutting-edge AI capabilities.

B. Modular and Composable Models

Future LLMs will adopt modular designs, enabling specialized components to handle different tasks. These modular systems allow for:

- Efficient retraining of specific components without modifying the entire model.
- Easier integration of domain-specific knowledge.

Example: A modular LLM might include distinct components for medical terminology, legal reasoning, and financial analysis, each fine-tuned independently.

C. Multimodal Mastery

Building on the foundation of multimodal models like OpenAI's CLIP and Google's Flamingo, the next wave of LLMs will seamlessly integrate text, images, audio, and video. These systems will:

- Understand and generate content across multiple formats.
- Power applications like video summarization, interactive virtual agents, and immersive AR/VR experiences.

Case in Point: Imagine an AI that analyzes a video conference, generates a summary in text, identifies key topics visually displayed, and highlights critical audio cues—all in real time.

2. Energy Efficiency and Sustainability

A. Low-Carbon AI

The environmental impact of training and deploying LLMs has raised concerns, driving research into energy-efficient solutions. Future innovations will focus on reducing the carbon footprint of LLMs through:

- **Green AI Frameworks:** Training systems using renewable energy and optimizing data center operations.
- **Quantization Techniques:** Reducing model precision (e.g., from float32 to int8) to decrease energy consumption during training and inference.

Example Innovation: OpenAI and Microsoft's collaboration on sustainable AI infrastructure is a step toward developing low-carbon AI models.

B. Federated Training

Federated learning, where models are trained collaboratively across decentralized devices without sharing raw data, will become a cornerstone of energy-efficient AI. By leveraging distributed resources, federated training reduces the need for massive centralized data centers.

Benefits:

- Privacy-preserving computation.
- Lower energy consumption through edge-based training.

3. Personalized and Adaptive AI

A. Hyper-Personalization

Next-generation LLMs will deliver highly personalized user experiences by adapting to individual preferences, contexts, and goals. Through continuous learning, these models will:

- Offer tailored recommendations.
- Adjust their communication styles based on user interactions.

Example Application: An AI-driven writing assistant that learns a user's tone, style, and preferred vocabulary over time, enabling seamless collaboration.

B. Real-Time Learning

Real-time learning will allow LLMs to update their knowledge dynamically without requiring retraining on entire datasets. This capability will enable:

- Faster adaptation to evolving user needs.
- On-the-fly integration of new knowledge, such as breaking news or regulatory changes.

Implementation: Dynamic knowledge graphs integrated with LLMs will provide real-time context and updates, ensuring accuracy and relevance.

4. Enhanced Explainability and Interpretability

As LLMs are deployed in critical applications, such as healthcare and legal systems, explainability will become paramount. Innovations in interpretability will make AI systems more transparent and accountable.

A. Visualizing Attention Mechanisms

Advancements in visualizing attention maps will help users understand which parts of the input data influence model outputs. For instance:

- Heatmaps showing which words or phrases contributed most to a decision.
- Visual overlays on images to highlight areas of interest.

B. Counterfactual Analysis

LLMs will incorporate counterfactual reasoning, enabling users to ask "what if" questions to explore alternative scenarios. This capability will enhance trust and usability in decision-making systems.

Example: In a legal AI application, users could explore how changes in a set of facts might alter the outcome of a recommendation.

5. Autonomous AI Agents

A. Self-Improving Models

Future LLMs will incorporate self-supervised feedback loops, enabling them to improve their performance autonomously over time. By monitoring their own outputs and user feedback, these models will:

- Identify areas of weakness.
- Generate synthetic training data to refine their capabilities.

B. Task-Oriented AI Systems

LLMs will evolve from passive tools to active agents capable of completing complex tasks autonomously. By integrating with APIs, sensors, and other systems, these models will:

- Plan and execute multi-step processes.
- Monitor progress and adjust strategies dynamically.

Example Application: An AI-powered project manager that autonomously schedules tasks, tracks deadlines, and reallocates resources as priorities shift.

6. Democratization of AI Development

A. Open-Source Models

The rise of open-source LLMs will enable smaller organizations and individual developers to leverage state-of-the-art AI. Projects like Hugging Face's Transformers and Meta's LLaMA (Large Language Model Meta AI) are already setting the stage for widespread accessibility.

B. Low-Code and No-Code AI

Low-code platforms will empower non-technical users to create sophisticated AI applications by abstracting the complexity of model development. These platforms will offer:

- Drag-and-drop interfaces for model customization.
- Pre-built modules for common use cases, such as chatbots and sentiment analysis.

Impact: Democratizing AI development will foster innovation across industries, especially in small businesses and startups.

7. Ethical and Responsible AI

A. Proactive Bias Mitigation

Future models will incorporate automated mechanisms for detecting and mitigating bias during training and inference. These systems will:

- Regularly audit training data for bias.
- Flag potentially harmful outputs in real-time.

B. Secure AI Models

Enhanced security measures will protect LLMs from adversarial attacks and misuse. Innovations in this area include:

- Robust defenses against model poisoning and data manipulation.
- Secure enclaves for sensitive computations.

8. Real-World Applications of Emerging Innovations

A. Healthcare

Multimodal LLMs will analyze patient records, medical images, and real-time sensor data to deliver precise diagnostics and personalized treatment plans.

B. Autonomous Vehicles

Integrating vision, text, and sensor data, LLMs will power safer and more reliable autonomous navigation systems.

C. Creative Content Generation

AI-driven creative tools will produce multimedia content, blending text, images, and audio to create immersive storytelling experiences.

Conclusion

The innovations on the horizon for LLMs promise to reshape industries, enhance human capabilities, and address global challenges. From modular architectures and energy-efficient systems to hyper-personalized experiences and real-time adaptability, the future of LLMs is defined by versatility and responsibility. As these technologies continue to evolve, their successful integration into society will depend on balancing innovation with ethical considerations, ensuring that AI systems are equitable, transparent, and aligned with humanity's best interests. Through continued research, collaboration, and innovation, LLMs are poised to unlock a new era of intelligent solutions and transformative possibilities.

Conclusion

Chapter 13: Your Path Forward

Recap of Key Takeaways

As we conclude this exploration of large language models (LLMs), it's essential to distill the wealth of information covered into actionable insights. LLMs represent a transformative leap in artificial intelligence, reshaping how we process, interpret, and generate information. From foundational principles to advanced applications and emerging innovations, this book has equipped you with the knowledge to not only understand LLMs but also leverage them effectively.

In this chapter, we summarize the key takeaways from our journey through LLM engineering, revisiting foundational concepts, critical challenges, and practical strategies for deploying and optimizing these powerful tools. This recap will serve as a roadmap, reinforcing the core lessons and offering clarity on the path forward.

1. The Foundations of LLMs: A New Era in AI

Understanding the Basics

- LLMs are built on transformer architectures, leveraging self-attention mechanisms to process sequential data with unparalleled efficiency.
- They are trained on vast datasets using self-supervised learning, enabling them to capture nuanced patterns in text, code, and other modalities.

Core Architecture

- The transformer architecture lies at the heart of LLMs, with its encoder and decoder components facilitating tasks like language understanding, generation, and translation.
- Attention mechanisms allow LLMs to prioritize relevant information, making them adept at handling complex, context-dependent tasks.

2. Building and Fine-Tuning LLMs

Training Fundamentals

- Pretraining involves training a model on extensive, diverse datasets to develop a generalized understanding of language.
- Fine-tuning adapts pretrained models to specific tasks or domains, such as medical diagnosis or legal document summarization.

Optimization Strategies

- Techniques like parameter-efficient fine-tuning, quantization, and pruning allow developers to optimize models for performance and efficiency.
- Transfer learning enables LLMs to leverage knowledge from related tasks, reducing training time and resource requirements.

3. Practical Applications of LLMs

Core Use Cases

- LLMs have revolutionized natural language processing tasks, including text generation, sentiment analysis, and machine translation.
- Multimodal applications extend LLM capabilities to integrate text with images, audio, and video, unlocking new possibilities in areas like video captioning and conversational AI.

Industry Impact

- In healthcare, LLMs assist in diagnostics, treatment recommendations, and medical research.
- In education, they enable personalized learning experiences and real-time tutoring.
- Creative industries leverage LLMs for content generation, such as drafting scripts, designing graphics, and composing music.

4. Deploying LLMs for Real-World Impact

Infrastructure and Scalability

- Deploying LLMs requires robust infrastructure, often involving cloud-based solutions, GPUs, or TPUs to handle computational demands.
- Scalable systems integrate tools like Kubernetes and Docker to manage resources efficiently and enable smooth deployments.

Monitoring and Maintenance

- Continuous training and monitoring ensure that LLMs remain accurate and relevant over time. Techniques like data drift detection and feedback loops are critical for maintaining performance.

5. Overcoming Ethical Challenges

Bias and Fairness

- LLMs inherit biases from their training data, which can result in discriminatory outputs. Mitigating this requires careful dataset curation, fairness-aware algorithms, and regular audits.

Transparency and Accountability

- As black-box systems, LLMs often lack explainability, making it difficult to trace their decision-making processes. Advances in interpretability, such as attention visualization and counterfactual analysis, are addressing this gap.

Responsible AI

- Safeguards like access controls, content moderation, and regulatory compliance ensure that LLMs are deployed ethically and align with societal values.

6. Innovations and Future Trends

Emerging Architectures

- Sparse models and modular designs are paving the way for more efficient and specialized LLMs, reducing resource demands while expanding capabilities.

Multimodal Mastery

- The integration of vision, audio, and text is driving the development of unified models that process and generate content across multiple modalities.

Personalization and Adaptability

- Hyper-personalized AI systems that learn user preferences and dynamically adapt to new data are becoming a reality, enhancing user experiences.

7. Skills and Strategies for Working with LLMs

Key Technical Skills

- Mastering programming languages like Python and frameworks such as PyTorch or TensorFlow is essential for implementing and fine-tuning LLMs.
- Understanding machine learning fundamentals, including data preprocessing, optimization techniques, and evaluation metrics, is crucial.

Collaboration Across Domains

- LLMs are interdisciplinary tools, requiring collaboration between data scientists, domain experts, and software engineers to maximize their potential.

Continuous Learning

- Staying ahead in the rapidly evolving field of LLMs demands a commitment to continuous learning. Exploring research papers, attending AI conferences, and experimenting with open-source models are effective ways to stay updated.

8. Real-World Examples: Success Stories and Lessons Learned

Healthcare Revolution

- In healthcare, LLMs have been deployed to analyze medical literature, identify potential drug interactions, and assist in radiological diagnostics. These applications demonstrate the transformative impact of LLMs when paired with domain-specific expertise.

Customer Support Automation

- Companies are leveraging LLMs to power chatbots and virtual assistants that deliver seamless, 24/7 customer support. These systems enhance user satisfaction while reducing operational costs.

Content Creation at Scale

- LLMs are enabling businesses to scale content production, from generating marketing copy to creating interactive educational materials. This capability underscores the versatility of LLMs across creative domains.

9. Challenges and Opportunities Ahead

Computational Costs

- The high computational demands of training and deploying LLMs remain a challenge. Innovations in energy-efficient architectures and federated learning are addressing these concerns.

Regulatory Landscape

- As LLMs influence critical industries, regulatory frameworks must evolve to ensure transparency, accountability, and compliance with privacy laws.

Ethical AI

- Balancing innovation with ethical considerations will be key to ensuring that LLMs serve humanity responsibly and equitably.

10. Your Role in the Future of LLMs

The knowledge gained from this book positions you to contribute meaningfully to the field of LLMs, whether as a developer, researcher, or strategist. By understanding the technical foundations, ethical imperatives, and practical applications of LLMs, you are equipped to:

- Build scalable and impactful AI solutions.
- Navigate the ethical complexities of AI development.
- Innovate at the intersection of technology and societal needs.

Final Thoughts

The rise of large language models represents a defining moment in the evolution of artificial intelligence. As these systems continue to advance, their potential to solve complex problems, enhance human creativity, and drive global progress is boundless. However, realizing this potential requires a deep understanding of their capabilities, limitations, and ethical implications.

By recapping the key takeaways from this journey, we hope to empower you to harness the transformative power of LLMs responsibly and effectively. Whether you are deploying LLMs in your organization, pursuing research in AI, or exploring creative applications, the knowledge you've gained will serve as a foundation for innovation and impact in the rapidly evolving world of AI.

Tips for Continuous Learning and Staying Ahead

In the ever-evolving world of large language models (LLMs) and artificial intelligence (AI), staying current is not just a matter of choice; it's a necessity for those who want to excel in this dynamic field. With rapid advancements, emerging technologies, and shifting industry needs, a commitment to continuous learning is the cornerstone of success. This chapter offers actionable tips and strategies for keeping your skills sharp, staying informed, and remaining competitive as LLMs continue to transform industries.

1. Embrace a Lifelong Learning Mindset

A. Cultivate Curiosity

Continuous learning starts with curiosity. AI and LLMs are multifaceted fields with a constant influx of new research, tools, and techniques. Cultivating a genuine interest in exploring these developments will keep you engaged and motivated.

- **Actionable Step:** Dedicate time weekly to explore emerging trends, whether by reading research papers, following thought leaders on platforms like LinkedIn, or participating in AI forums.

B. Stay Open to Change

The field of AI evolves quickly, often rendering previously dominant tools or methods obsolete. Adaptability is key to navigating this landscape.

- **Example:** Transitioning from recurrent neural networks (RNNs) to transformers was a significant shift in AI research. Professionals who stayed open to this change were better positioned to capitalize on new opportunities.

2. Leverage Online Learning Resources

A. Explore MOOCs and Online Courses

Massive Open Online Courses (MOOCs) provide structured learning opportunities from top institutions and companies.

- **Top Platforms:**

- **Coursera:** Offers courses like "Natural Language Processing with Attention Models" by DeepLearning.AI.
- **edX:** Hosts advanced courses on AI and machine learning, often from universities like MIT or Stanford.
- **Udemy:** Features practical, hands-on courses for specific tools and frameworks.

B. Take Advantage of Free Tutorials

Open-source communities and companies often provide free tutorials and resources.

- **Examples:**
    - Hugging Face's blog posts and tutorials on implementing LLMs.
    - TensorFlow's and PyTorch's official documentation and hands-on guides.

C. Earn Certifications

Certifications in AI, machine learning, or cloud platforms (e.g., AWS Certified Machine Learning Specialty) can validate your expertise and enhance your resume.

3. Engage with Research and Publications

A. Read Academic Papers

Cutting-edge AI techniques are often introduced in academic papers. Platforms like arXiv host thousands of preprints on topics such as LLMs, transformer architectures, and optimization strategies.

- **Actionable Step:** Follow conferences like NeurIPS, ACL, and ICML to access the latest research. Summarize papers in layman's terms to reinforce understanding.

B. Follow Industry Blogs and Newsletters

Stay informed about practical advancements and industry applications by subscribing to trusted AI blogs and newsletters.

- **Examples:**
    - The Gradient
    - Distill.pub
    - Papers with Code

C. Use AI to Learn About AI

Leverage tools like ChatGPT or other LLMs to summarize research papers, explain complex concepts, or even recommend resources tailored to your learning needs.

4. Build and Experiment

A. Start Small, but Build Often

Hands-on practice is one of the most effective ways to deepen your understanding of LLMs. Begin with small projects that allow you to implement concepts you've learned.

- **Project Ideas:**
    - Build a chatbot using Hugging Face transformers.
    - Fine-tune a pretrained model on a custom dataset, such as product reviews or medical records.
    - Develop a sentiment analysis tool for social media data.

B. Contribute to Open-Source Projects

Contributing to open-source projects not only enhances your technical skills but also expands your network within the AI community.

- **Actionable Step:** Explore repositories on GitHub related to LLMs, such as Hugging Face Transformers or OpenAI's tools. Start with documentation improvements or small bug fixes.

C. Build a Portfolio

Document your projects and share them on platforms like GitHub or personal websites. A well-curated portfolio demonstrates your expertise and can be instrumental in career advancement.

5. Stay Connected with the Community

A. Join AI Communities

Networking with peers, mentors, and experts fosters collaboration and keeps you informed about industry trends.

- **Recommended Communities:**
    - AI-focused Discord servers and Slack groups.
    - Forums like Reddit's r/MachineLearning or Stack Overflow.
    - Meetup groups for AI enthusiasts in your area.

B. Attend Conferences and Workshops

Participating in conferences like NeurIPS, CVPR, or the AI Summit allows you to engage with cutting-edge research and industry leaders.

- **Pro Tip:** Many conferences offer virtual attendance options, making them accessible even if you cannot attend in person.

C. Share Knowledge

Teaching others is one of the best ways to solidify your understanding. Write blog posts, record tutorials, or present at local meetups to share your insights.

6. Explore Emerging Tools and Frameworks

A. Experiment with New Frameworks

LLM development is supported by a growing ecosystem of tools and frameworks. Staying updated with these can enhance your productivity and effectiveness.

- **Examples:**
    - **Hugging Face Transformers:** Widely used for implementing LLMs.
    - **LangChain:** Designed for building applications with LLMs.
    - **TensorFlow and PyTorch:** Core frameworks for deep learning.

B. Embrace MLOps

MLOps tools streamline the deployment and monitoring of AI models, an increasingly important skill as AI systems move into production.

- **Popular Tools:**
    - MLflow for tracking experiments.
    - Kubeflow for orchestrating machine learning workflows.

C. Stay Agile with Cloud Platforms

Cloud services like AWS, Azure, and Google Cloud offer scalable resources for training and deploying LLMs. Familiarity with these platforms is invaluable for real-world applications.

7. Balance Depth and Breadth

A. Develop Domain Expertise

While LLMs are versatile, applying them effectively often requires domain-specific knowledge. Choose a field that aligns with your interests—healthcare, finance, or entertainment—and deepen your expertise in that area.

B. Stay Broadly Informed

Maintain a general awareness of trends and developments in AI beyond LLMs. Understanding related areas, such as computer vision, reinforcement learning, or edge computing, provides a holistic perspective.

8. Emphasize Soft Skills

A. Communication and Collaboration

As LLMs are interdisciplinary, clear communication with team members across domains is essential. Practice explaining complex technical concepts in simple terms.

B. Problem-Solving

Employ creative problem-solving techniques to adapt LLMs to new challenges. Break down complex issues into smaller, manageable parts.

C. Ethical Awareness

As LLMs gain influence, understanding ethical considerations—such as bias mitigation, privacy, and transparency—will become increasingly important.

9. Seek Mentorship and Guidance

A. Identify Mentors

Connect with professionals in the field who can provide guidance, share experiences, and offer career advice.

B. Participate in Mentorship Programs

Many organizations and online communities offer mentorship programs specifically for AI practitioners.

C. Be Open to Feedback

Constructive criticism is invaluable for growth. Actively seek feedback on your projects, ideas, and approaches.

10. Future-Proof Your Skills

A. Monitor Trends

Stay ahead by anticipating shifts in AI research and industry needs. Subscribe to trend analyses, white papers, and reports from leading AI companies.

B. Innovate and Adapt

Innovation stems from curiosity and creativity. Experiment with unconventional applications of LLMs and push the boundaries of what they can achieve.

C. Invest in Lifelong Learning

Allocate time and resources for learning throughout your career. The willingness to learn continuously will keep you competitive in this fast-paced industry.

Conclusion

The journey to mastering LLMs and staying at the forefront of AI is not a destination but an ongoing process. By embracing curiosity, leveraging the wealth of available resources, engaging with the community, and honing your skills, you can position yourself as a leader in this transformative field. Remember, the key to staying ahead lies not only in technical expertise but also in adaptability, collaboration, and ethical awareness. With these strategies, you are well-equipped to navigate the ever-changing AI landscape and make meaningful contributions to the future of technology.

Leveraging LLM Skills for Career Growth

The transformative power of large language models (LLMs) has reshaped industries, creating opportunities for professionals with the skills to develop, deploy, and optimize these systems. Whether you are an engineer, data scientist, researcher, or entrepreneur, mastering LLMs can open doors to new roles, projects, and innovations. However, success in this competitive field requires more than just technical expertise; it demands a strategic approach to career development, leveraging your LLM skills to stay relevant and thrive.

This chapter explores how to harness your knowledge of LLMs for career growth, offering actionable insights on identifying opportunities, building a strong professional presence, and positioning yourself as a leader in the evolving AI landscape.

1. Understanding the Demand for LLM Expertise

A. Industries Driving Demand

LLMs have applications across diverse sectors, making expertise in this field highly sought after. Key industries include:

- **Technology and Software Development:** Powering chatbots, recommendation systems, and code generation tools.
- **Healthcare:** Assisting in diagnostics, medical research, and patient communication.
- **Finance:** Automating document analysis, fraud detection, and customer support.
- **Education:** Enabling personalized learning and automated grading systems.
- **Creative Arts and Media:** Generating content, enhancing storytelling, and streamlining video production.

B. Roles for LLM Professionals

Professionals skilled in LLMs can pursue roles such as:

- AI Engineer or Machine Learning Engineer
- Data Scientist specializing in NLP
- AI Product Manager
- Research Scientist in LLM innovation
- Technical Consultant for AI-powered solutions

2. Building a Strong Foundation in LLMs

A. Develop a Comprehensive Skill Set

To succeed in roles involving LLMs, focus on mastering key technical and conceptual areas:

1. **Core AI Fundamentals:**
    - Machine learning basics (supervised, unsupervised, and reinforcement learning).
    - Understanding neural networks, transformers, and attention mechanisms.
2. **Programming Proficiency:**
    - Python is the industry standard, with libraries like TensorFlow and PyTorch being essential.
    - Familiarity with NLP-specific tools such as Hugging Face, spaCy, and NLTK.
3. **Data Management:**
    - Skills in data preprocessing, tokenization, and embeddings.
    - Experience with vector databases and knowledge retrieval systems.
4. **Deployment and Optimization:**
    - Knowledge of MLOps, including tools like MLflow and Kubernetes.
    - Familiarity with cloud platforms such as AWS, Azure, and Google Cloud.

B. Pursue Certifications and Advanced Training

Certifications demonstrate expertise and commitment to professional growth. Consider:

- **Machine Learning Specializations:** Offered by Coursera, DeepLearning.AI, and edX.
- **Cloud Certifications:** AWS Machine Learning Specialty or Google Cloud AI Engineer.
- **NLP-Specific Training:** Hugging Face certifications or Stanford's NLP specialization.

3. Creating a Portfolio to Showcase Expertise

A. Build and Share Projects

A portfolio of practical projects can demonstrate your ability to apply LLM knowledge effectively. Include:

1. **Real-World Applications:**
    - A chatbot for customer support using GPT-based models.
    - A text summarization tool for legal or academic documents.
2. **Innovative Use Cases:**
    - Fine-tuning an LLM on domain-specific datasets.
    - Developing a RAG pipeline for real-time information retrieval.
3. **Open-Source Contributions:**
    - Improve documentation, fix bugs, or add features to popular repositories like Hugging Face Transformers.

B. Document Your Work

Ensure your portfolio includes detailed explanations of your projects, including:

- The problem addressed.
- Technologies and methodologies used.
- Challenges overcome and outcomes achieved.

Pro Tip: Host your portfolio on platforms like GitHub, or create a personal website to showcase your expertise.

4. Networking and Building a Professional Presence

A. Join AI Communities

Engage with AI-focused communities to learn from peers, share insights, and discover opportunities. Popular options include:

- **Online Forums:** Reddit's r/MachineLearning, AI Stack Exchange.
- **Slack Channels:** AI-focused workspaces like the MLOps community.

B. Attend Industry Events

Participate in conferences, webinars, and hackathons to stay informed about the latest trends and connect with industry leaders. Key events include:

- NeurIPS, CVPR, and ACL for academic insights.
- AI Summit and O'Reilly AI Conference for industry perspectives.

C. Share Your Knowledge

Position yourself as an expert by contributing to the AI ecosystem:

- Write blog posts on platforms like Medium or Substack.
- Create tutorials or video content on YouTube.
- Present at meetups or local tech events.

5. Identifying Career Opportunities

A. Target High-Growth Companies

Focus on organizations that are heavily investing in AI, such as:

- Tech giants (e.g., Google, Microsoft, OpenAI).
- AI startups working on cutting-edge innovations.
- Companies in industries undergoing digital transformation.

B. Leverage Job Boards and Platforms

Explore specialized AI job boards like AI-Jobs.net, or general platforms like LinkedIn and Indeed, for opportunities tailored to LLM professionals.

C. Stay Open to Freelance and Consulting Roles

Freelance platforms like Toptal or Upwork are excellent for gaining diverse experience and building a network of industry contacts.

6. Advancing Within Your Current Role

A. Apply LLMs to Solve Business Problems

Even if your role isn't AI-focused, identify ways to integrate LLMs into your work:

- Automate repetitive tasks using text generation or summarization tools.
- Enhance decision-making with AI-driven insights.

B. Advocate for AI Initiatives

Propose AI-driven projects within your organization, such as:

- Developing a chatbot for internal or external communication.
- Using LLMs to analyze large datasets or generate reports.

C. Upskill Your Team

Share your LLM knowledge by leading workshops or creating training materials for colleagues. Demonstrating leadership in this area can position you for promotions or leadership roles.

7. Staying Ahead in a Competitive Field

A. Monitor Emerging Trends

Stay informed about advancements in AI research, such as:

- Sparse models and modular architectures.
- Multimodal systems that combine text, vision, and audio.
- Real-time learning and dynamic updates.

B. Experiment with Emerging Tools

Test and implement new frameworks and libraries as they emerge. Being an early adopter can set you apart as a forward-thinking professional.

C. Collaborate Across Disciplines

LLMs intersect with fields like biology, law, and the arts. Collaborating with domain experts can lead to unique and impactful applications.

8. Long-Term Career Strategies

A. Set Clear Goals

Define your career aspirations, whether they involve becoming a technical expert, leading AI projects, or launching your own startup.

B. Pursue Leadership Roles

As you gain experience, consider transitioning into roles that allow you to shape AI strategies, such as:

- AI Architect or Chief AI Officer.
- Director of Data Science or Machine Learning.

C. Explore Entrepreneurship

LLMs offer immense potential for creating innovative startups. Identify gaps in the market and leverage your expertise to build solutions.

Example Opportunities:

- AI-powered tools for niche industries (e.g., legal tech, education).
- Customizable LLMs for small and medium-sized businesses.

9. Cultivating Soft Skills for Career Growth

A. Communication

Effectively articulate technical concepts to non-technical stakeholders, bridging the gap between AI and business goals.

B. Problem-Solving

Approach challenges creatively, leveraging LLMs to find efficient and impactful solutions.

C. Ethical Awareness

Demonstrate a strong understanding of ethical considerations, positioning yourself as a responsible AI practitioner.

Conclusion

Leveraging your LLM skills for career growth requires a combination of technical expertise, strategic thinking, and proactive engagement with the AI community. By building a strong foundation, showcasing your abilities, and seizing opportunities to innovate, you can position yourself as a leader in this transformative field. Whether you aim to excel in an established organization, drive change as an entrepreneur, or contribute to groundbreaking research, the future of AI offers limitless potential for those prepared to navigate its challenges and opportunities.

FREE SUPPLEMENTARY RESOURCES

☑ LLM REAL WORLD SCENARIOS
☑ LLM SOLUTIONS AND CODE EXAMPLES

SCAN THE QR CODE TO DOWNLOAD

COMPLEMENTARY RESOURCES

Why Your Support Matters for This Book:

Creating this book has been an unexpectedly tough journey, more so than even the most complex coding sessions. For the first time, I've faced the daunting challenge of writer's block. While I understand the subject matter, translating it into clear, logical, and engaging writing is another matter altogether.
Moreover, my choice to bypass traditional publishers has led me to embrace the role of an 'independent author.' This path has had its hurdles, yet my commitment to helping others remains strong.
This is why your feedback on Amazon would be incredibly valuable. Your thoughts and opinions not only matter greatly to me, but they also play a crucial role in spreading the word about this book. Here's what I suggest:

1. **If you haven't done so already, scan the QR code at the beginning of the book to download the FREE SUPPLEMENTARY RESOURCES.**

2. **Scan the QR code below and quickly leave feedback on Amazon!**

The optimal approach? Consider making a brief video to share your impressions of the book! If that's a bit much, don't worry at all. Just leaving a feedback and including a few photos of the book would be fantastic too!

Note: There's no obligation whatsoever, but it would be immensely valued!

I'm thrilled to embark on this journey with you. Are you prepared to delve in?
Enjoy your reading!

Made in United States
Troutdale, OR
03/18/2025